TURKISH FIRE

**STREET FOOD AND BARBECUE
FROM THE WILD HEART OF TURKEY**

TURKISH FIRE

STREET FOOD AND BARBECUE
FROM THE WILD HEART OF TURKEY

SEVTAP YÜCE

hardie grant books

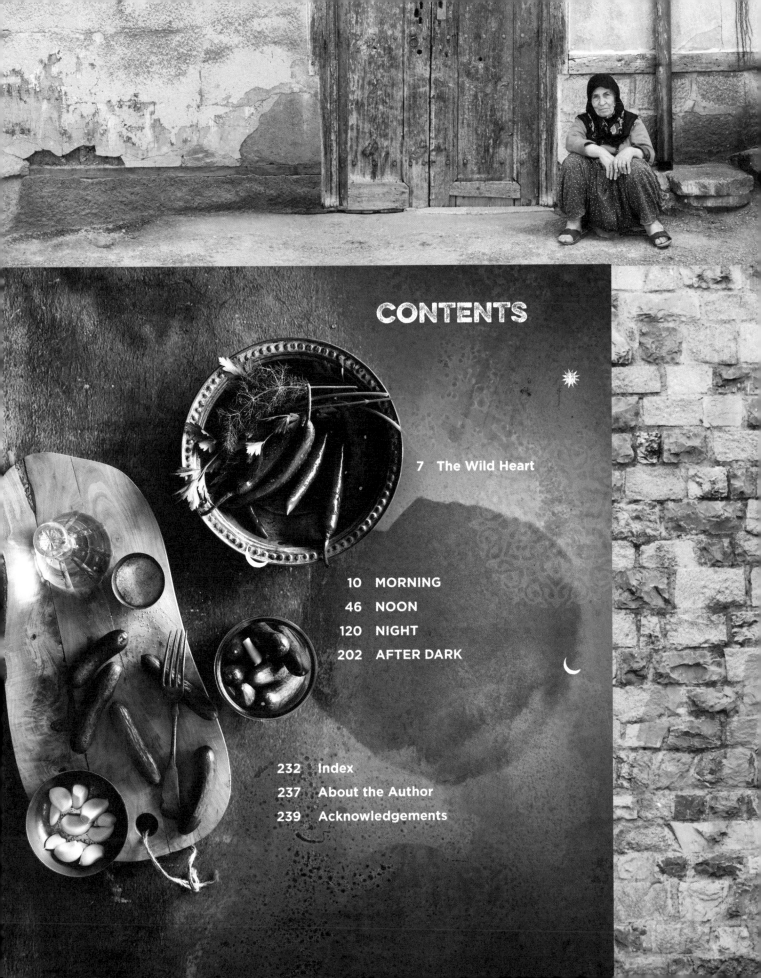

CONTENTS

THE WILD HEART

The weather is getting colder. My father buys a ton of wood and two tons of coal and we hope this will be enough to last us all winter.

It is time to get the *soba* ready. Our *soba* sat in the living room. You might call it a pot-belly stove, but I call it a top-belly stove, with a round opening on the top to feed the wood and coal through. My mother would get up early in the morning and light the fire and place the *çaydanlık* — a large teapot — on top, full of water. After that she would prepare the breakfast and get us ready for school. The fire would burn all day to keep the house warm and give us a warm home to return to. At the end of the busy day the fire would burn bright enough to make roasted chestnuts on top for our after-dinner treat. Mum would be sure to cut a sliver from the nut so it didn't explode while cooking. When the nuts were brown enough, we had to take them from the *soba* and peel them hot, to make sure the second skin came away easily. Pop them into your mouth and yummmm.

In those cold days of winter, fire was part of every Turkish home.

In the warm days of spring and summer, we would go on picnics, and still the fire was at the centre of it all. For us, going on a picnic didn't mean just packing a basket. We had to load the car (a big black and red Chevrolet) with the *küçük tüp* (a small camping gas burner), the *mangal* (a barbecue), the *çaydanlık*, plastic bottles for collecting fresh spring water, all the meat, all the salads, the plates and tea and, of course, a bottle of *rakı*. It all goes into the car — sisters, brothers, with the cutlery, the blankets — and off we'd go. We would drive for an hour or two to find a *pınar*, a freshwater spring, and park the car under the shade of a big tree.

Out would come the blankets and plates, cutlery, glasses and our food. We would turn on the car radio and listen to music, and my father would take charge of the barbecue. (It's not so different here in Australia!) We would make the salads; Turks love their salads. We'd chop everything into bite-sized pieces — the tomatoes, the green peppers, sweet tender cucumbers, the flat-leaf parsley, then add a little lemon juice and a drizzle of olive oil. The adults would drink some *rakı* ... maybe drink-driving was not such an offence in those days.

The *rakı* gets poured, the fire burns.

My father would cook the meat, and I have to tell you it was amazing. We would eat, laugh and cry. And then we would fill up the plastic bottles from the *pınar* and take the water home for our tea. Oh my god, those teas — I have never tasted the same. All the food, all the meat, all the salads, never tasted the same.

Maybe those experiences made me who I am, made me so deeply involved with food, which I would like to share with you from the bottom of my heart. Probably that is why I love cooking and sharing every little mouthful. I could never sit at a table with a whole plate just to myself, without saying, *Taste this, what do you think? I think you are going to love it ...* Those experiences also gave me skills to survive for the rest of my life. So when I look at a piece of meat today, or a tomato, or an eggplant, I smile and my imagination goes wild. Oh my god, what can I make with these beautiful treasures? I might chop the eggplant, fry it in a little olive oil, add some tomatoes, salt, pepper, and a whole lot of love.

Back then, at those family barbecues, my father — my *baba* — would be the one to light the fire, the one to cook the meat, to drive the car, to get us home.

Kamber Yüce, my *baba*, was born in 1937 in Çorum, a small village four hours north of Ankara. One of six boys, and one sister. Their father, my grandfather, supported the family by grinding the villagers' wheat. The people of the village would collect the wheat from the fields, boil it and bring it to my grandfather, and he would grind it on a big, round stone to make cracked wheat — what we call today burghul, or *bulgur*. He would take the husks off on a big stone and walk his big horse around and around and around. He would smoke constantly, like a chimney — so he kept the fire going, even while he was working. They would all sit down for dinner, all on the floor — the father, the mother, six boys and the girl. The food would be served on a tray, with flat bread used as a spoon, in a small shovel shape. They would have a little meat, and some vegetables grown by my grandmother, Zülpi. My father said if he really liked the dish, he would pretend to spit on the food; his brothers and sister would pull away and he could eat the rest of the meal in peace.

He told me that one day he came across a bunch of women who were making bread. He was so hungry he stole a piece of bread off them and tried to run away. One of the women was so angry she started chasing him, then she threw a knife and it hit him on the shoulder. That was probably the only thing he ever stole in his life, but my father said it was worth it, because the bread tasted so good! Even though he had such a hungry fire in his belly, he was the most decent human being I've ever met, and became an honest, hardworking breadwinner ... rather than a bread-pincher!

When Kamber was seventeen, he fell in love with a beautiful young girl, Hatice. They married and had my beautiful sister, Güfer. They started up a little corner store, the Yüce Bakkalı, and lived next door,

surrounded by cherry trees, apple trees, pear trees — any tree that was in the garden was beautiful, and bore edible fruit. And they were in love.

Hatice fell pregnant again, but died in childbirth, when Güfer was just two years old. The hospital told my father that not only did he lose his beautiful wife, but also his baby daughter. He was devastated. The only thing that kept him going was my lovely sister.

Some time after his beloved Hatice passed away, Kamber met my mother, Makbule. She was sixteen and he was twenty-seven. A few years later, I was born. He always wanted to have a son — then my brother Murat was born, two years after me. And my brother Ferhat two years later. (Obviously my parents had something about two years.)

When we were growing up, my father was the sole breadwinner, and provided everything we needed. In those days women stayed home and looked after the children, cleaned the house, and prepared food for the harsh winter to come. In the early days of my childhood my *baba* sold fruit and vegetables. I remember him bringing home the most amazing peaches, which I still have never tasted anything like. Some nights after work he would bring home the most beautifully roasted spatchcock — just one, mind you. Oh my god, it tasted so good. You may be sitting there thinking, how can one spatchcock feed a family of six? But it did and it tasted incredible.

Later my *baba* also had a *kahvane*, or café. Back in those days, about forty years ago, only the men went to a *kahvane*, to play backgammon and drink endless cups of tea. Life was good.

Then my father's favourite brother, Haşim, was killed when he was thirty-one. When Haşim died, my father had to take over responsibility for Haşim's *taverna*.

(In the *taverna* would be a lot of meat dishes from the fire, some beer, maybe some *rakı*, a lot of music. There are amazing dishes from his time at the *taverna* that I will share with you a little later on, if you hold your horses ...) As well as looking after Haṣim's *taverna*, my father also had to look after Haṣim's wife, and their two daughters and son, as well as his own family.

Perhaps those were the days that put more wrinkles on his forehead, and why he came home at night and smoked endless cigarettes and drank countless cups of tea.

Just twelve months after his brother's death, we were about to go for a picnic with the whole family and all our relatives. But *baba* had a stroke. He couldn't move his left side. We fed him a lot of garlic, lovely yoghurt, and no salt. We loved him to bits, and he got better. We had a very happy family; my sister married and had a son, Volkan, who *baba* adored; *baba* even shaved Volkan's eyebrows, so they would grow into strong Turkish eyebrows. Today Volkan has amazing eyebrows, but not much hair on top. And now he has a son and a daughter, my father's great-grandchildren.

In 1985, my father decided to visit his parents in Çorum, and to take my brother Murat with him. While he was there, my *baba* had a massive heart attack, and he died. He wasn't even fifty — so young. Sadly, my brother Murat was also taken away too young. He was kidnapped and executed in Iraq on 2 August 2004, the day before his thirty-fifth birthday, leaving behind twin boys and a daughter. I miss him so much.

My father was the most fiery, most honest, and most kind man I have ever known. Oh my god, I have to tell you, did he have fire.

I wish I could sit with him now. I remember him sitting there those nights, smoking endless cigarettes, drinking countless cups of tea. I wish I had known what was in his mind. Was he worried about how we would light the next fire, or what we would eat next? I wish he could answer all my questions, and I wish I had all the answers for them.

But all I have is memories of cherry trees, pears, apples, and the juice of the most beautiful peaches I've ever tasted in my life running down my arms.

I suppose my father passed on a lot of things. One of the things he passed on to me was his passion. That fire still lives in my belly and, hey, we all know how fiery the Turks are! Now you know where it begins.

I was still a teenager when my father passed away. But time goes by, and I married and moved to Australia. Years later I wrote my first cookbook, *Turkish Flavours*, and then my second cookbook, *Turkish Meze* ... and then I thought, hey, I will take you all back to where it all started. Show you where I came from, show you what it was like.

And so I went back to Turkey, and to the city of Ankara, where I grew up.

I went back to where our old house once stood, only to find there were only three walls left standing. There was nothing left.

But where the *soba* used to be, where my mother lit the fire every morning, every winter's day, there were three women, sitting on the floor of my old house. One had the fire burning, sitting where the *soba* was, making bread with the others, to feed their family.

After all these years, the fire still burned.

MORNING

If you would like to create a traditional Turkish breakfast, I can tell you how my family did it.

Whoever got up first would put the pot on for the tea. One person would be sent to the bakery with a few coins to pick up a few loaves of hot crusty bread. This person would most likely be the smallest kid; in my family that was me.

With the leftover money I would buy myself some chocolate. When I'd return home with the bread, my mum would ask me for the change. I would say there wasn't any, and then she'd say she'd check with the bakery! I'd be so scared, thinking maybe I had tell-tale chocolate stains on my face ...

In the meantime, someone would set the table with bowls of olives, plates of sliced tomatoes, bowls of parsley and sliced cucumber, a plate of green chillies. There would always be a few different cheeses, some hard, some soft, like *beyaz peynir*, a soft white cheese like feta. One cheese, called *dil peyniri*, would be pulled apart to make strands, like thick hair. There would also be butter, honey and different jams. (Whenever there was an abundance of fruit, jam would be made. When the strawberries were everywhere, so was the jam. There would be peach jam, then quince jam, then sour cherry jam, plum jam ... It's like there was a jam for all seasons!)

In the centre of the table would be a big hot dish of eggs, boiled or cooked in ways I will show you in this book.

There would be small tea glasses and bowls of sugar cubes, with teaspoons already in the glasses. The first weak tea was poured for the young ones, with the strong tea given to the older ones.

Each person would have a plate in front of them, and they could choose whatever they wanted from the many, many delights on the table.

Then my mum would do a stocktake of the breakfast ingredients and tell Dad what we needed — maybe it was cheese and olives — and he would have to go to the special breakfast-goods shops.

Hopefully I will take you there one day ...

When I was a little girl, my father ran a *kahvane*, which translates into English as 'coffee house' — even though there was much more tea drunk there than coffee. As a little girl I would go around delivering tea to the nearby shops, dressed like a little boy.

Every household would have a *çaydanlık*, a special two-tiered teapot, made of steel. Here is how you use one to make a nice cup of Turkish tea.

ÇAY

TEA

2–3 tablespoons fine black tea leaves
sugar cubes, to serve

Fill the bottom teapot with cold water. In the smaller pot on top, put the tea leaves, then pour a splash of cold water over the leaves. Place the whole pot over a high heat.

When the water comes to the boil, pour the hot water from the bottom pot over the tea leaves on top.

Refill the bottom pot with cold water, turn the heat down to low, and wait until all the leaves have settled to the bottom of the top pot. This could take 5–10 minutes.

Into each small Turkish tea glass we pour about 1 cm (½ inch) of the brewed tea from the top pot, then top each glass up with hot water from the bottom pot.

Tea is always served with cubes of sugar.

When you hear the call '*Çargı, Çargı!*', you know your tea is coming.

You can see Turks love their pickles, every season of the year.

Quinces are the oldest fruit. Some people call quinces the 'goddess of love' fruit; I think they are not wrong! I love to bake them, poach them, and especially to make jam from them.

This is one of my favourite jams for breakfast. I love this jam folded through yoghurt, or spread on toasted, thinly sliced Turkish bread with fresh ricotta.

If you are into cheese platters, this jam is perfect with your favourite cheeses.

AYVA REÇELİ

QUINCE JAM

1 kg (2 lb 3 oz) quinces
1 kg (2 lb 3 oz) caster
   (superfine) sugar
juice of 1 lemon

Peel and core the quinces, then chop them into small pieces. Place in a stainless-steel saucepan with the sugar, lemon juice and 500 ml (17 fl oz/2 cups) water and mix together well.

Bring to the boil, then reduce the heat to a simmer and cook for 45–60 minutes, stirring occasionally to stop the mixture catching on the bottom of the pan. If it starts to catch, reduce the heat.

Using a tablespoon, remove a portion of the mixture and pour a little onto a cold plate. Allow to cool, then check for consistency — when you run your finger through the jam, it should leave a trail in the jam. If it doesn't, cook the jam a little longer.

Pour the hot jam into sterilised jars. Seal and store until you are ready to enjoy your jam — or give to very grateful friends, like me.

MAKES 1.5 KG (3 LB 5 OZ), ENOUGH TO FILL SIX 250 ML (8½ FL OZ) JARS

Sucuk is a spicy beef sausage, which can be seen hanging in shop windows everywhere in Turkey. You can barbecue these sausages, pan-fry them, or use them in a Turkish pide (see page 53).

SUCUKLU YUMURTA

SPICY TURKISH SAUSAGE WITH EGGS

100 g (3½ oz) sucuk
   (spicy beef sausage)
20 g (¾ oz) butter
6 free-range eggs
pul biber (see note), for sprinkling
crusty bread, to serve

Peel the skin off the sausage, then thinly slice the meat. Heat a frying pan and melt the butter. Cook the sausage over a high heat for 2–3 minutes on each side.

Crack the eggs on top and cook to your heart's desire; I like my eggs soft and runny, which usually takes 2–3 minutes.

Sprinkle with pul biber and serve warm, with crusty bread.

SERVES 3–4

NOTE

Pul biber is a crushed red powder made from dried aleppo peppers. It is mild to medium in heat, and the Turkish love sprinkling it over just about anything. If you can't find it in spice shops or Middle Eastern grocery stores, you can use chilli flakes instead.

Turks can't live without parsley. There's no curly parsley in Turkey, so please only use flat-leaf parsley, full of love.

This is another beautiful way to enjoy eggs. My mum sometimes made this for breakfast; at other times she made it for lunch.

MAYDANOZLU YUMURTA

BOILED EGG SALAD WITH PARSLEY

4 free-range eggs, at room
  temperature
30 g (1 oz/1 cup) finely chopped
  flat-leaf (Italian) parsley
65 g (2¼ oz/1 cup) thinly sliced
  spring onions (scallions)
60 g (2 oz/½ cup) chopped walnuts
125 ml (4 fl oz/½ cup) extra virgin
  olive oil
crusty bread or flat bread,
  to serve

Put the eggs in a saucepan. Pour in plenty of water and bring to the boil. Cook at a gentle boil for 8–10 minutes; in this recipe the eggs should be hard-boiled, but don't go mad. Let's not boil them too hard!

In a serving bowl, mix together the parsley, spring onion, walnuts and olive oil. Season with sea salt and freshly ground black pepper.

Peel the eggs and chop into chunks, then mix gently into the salad.

Serve with bread of your choice.

SERVES 4

People from the Black Sea are famous for their *hamsi*, fresh anchovies — one of Turkey's favourite fish. I also love the way they cook their eggs. You can have this particular dish for breakfast or lunch.

KARADENİZ AŞI

EGGS FROM THE BLACK SEA

3 free-range eggs
150 g (5½ oz) tasty
    cheddar, coarsely grated
40 g (1½ oz) butter
30 g (1 oz/¼ cup) yellow
    maize flour (see note)
1–2 tablespoons pul biber
    (see note, page 18)
crusty bread, to serve

Break the eggs into a bowl and add the cheese. Mix together well.

Melt the butter in a large frying pan over a medium heat. Add the maize flour and pul biber and mix into the melted butter. Season with sea salt. Cook for 5 minutes, constantly stirring, until the mixture is dry and crumbly.

Gradually add 375 ml (12½ fl oz/1½ cups) water and cook, stirring constantly, for a few minutes, until the mixture is the consistency of a thick sauce.

Spoon the egg and cheese mixture over the top, creating two layers. Then cover and cook for 6–8 minutes, until the egg and cheese mixture sets.

Serve warm, with crusty bread.

SERVES 3–4

NOTE

Maize flour is available in both yellow and white varieties. It is like a fine polenta, similar in texture to semolina flour. You will find it in Middle Eastern grocery stores and health food shops.

Pray for happiness and peace.

KAYGANA

EGGS COOKED IN MILK & SPRING ONION

6 free-range eggs
250 ml (8½ fl oz/1 cup) milk
75 g (2¾ oz/½ cup) plain
 (all-purpose) flour
20 g (¾ oz) butter
1 tablespoon pul biber (see note,
 page 18)
5 spring onions (scallions),
 finely chopped
diced tomatoes, to serve
crumbled Bulgarian feta, to serve

Crack the eggs into a bowl and lightly whisk. Add the milk and flour, season with sea salt and freshly ground black pepper and mix well.

Melt the butter in a large frying pan over a medium heat. Add half the spring onion and sprinkle with half the pul biber. Pour half the egg mixture over the top, then cover and cook until the eggs have set — about 5 minutes.

Remove the lid and place a large ceramic plate over the pan. Turn the pan over and slide the omelette onto the plate. Keep warm while cooking the remaining spring onion, pul biber and egg mixture in the same fashion as above.

Cut the omelettes into wedges and serve warm, scattered with some diced tomato and crumbled feta.

SERVES 4

This was one of my favourite breakfast dishes when I was growing up. Mum would simply serve it out of the frying pan, in the middle of our table. Back then we didn't have a dining table; instead we would sit on a *sofra*, a black and white cloth spread out on the ground. Mum would put a round wooden board with small legs in the middle of the cloth, and then rest a massive round copper tray, over a metre wide, on top of that. All the food would be served on this *tepsi* in this way, for breakfast, lunch and dinner.

This dish is another economical way of feeding four hungry people with just a handful of meat. You can adjust the amount of chillies to suit your taste. I like my egg yolks runny, served with very crusty bread, and with black tea to follow.

KIYMALI YUMURTA

EGGS COOKED IN MINCED LAMB

60 ml (2 fl oz/¼ cup) olive oil
1 brown onion, diced
3 green chillies, chopped
200 g (7 oz) minced (ground) lamb
2 vine-ripened tomatoes, diced
15 g (½ oz/½ cup) finely chopped
    flat-leaf (Italian) parsley
8 free-range eggs
crusty bread, to serve

Heat the olive oil in a large frying pan over a medium heat. Add the onion and fry for 6–8 minutes, or until soft.

Add the chilli and lamb and season with sea salt and freshly ground black pepper. Stir well to make sure the lamb doesn't form chunks. Cook for a few minutes, then stir in the tomato and parsley.

Spread the mixture evenly over the base of the pan. Using the back of a tablespoon, create eight shallow pockets in the lamb mixture, to hold the eggs. Now carefully crack an egg into each pocket. Cover and cook for about 5–6 minutes for a softly runny yolk, or until the eggs are cooked to your heart's desire.

Serve warm, with crusty bread.

SERVES 4–6

A friendly face in Ankara.

Turks love their chillies. Turkish chillies, *biber*, grow about 20 cm (8 inches) long, and range in heat from sweet to mildly hot. Turks eat their chillies for breakfast, lunch and dinner. You would not see a household without a bowl of green chillies on the table.

Once or twice a week, every neighbourhood will have a *pazar* (market), where the stallholders will come and gather so you can top up your supplies when your local shop, or *bakal*, is running low. When you go to the markets, you will buy lots of chillies. If one person in the household likes sweet chillies, you have to buy a kilo for them, and then a kilo of hot chillies for the others. I know this seems a lot to get your head around, but the chillies will disappear in no time.

If you don't like too much chilli, you can replace half the green chillies in this recipe with mild sweet banana peppers.

BİBERLİ YUMURTA

CHILLI EGGS

6 free-range eggs
1 tablespoon olive oil
40 g (1½ oz) butter
10 long green chillies, chopped
crusty bread, to serve

Crack the eggs into a bowl and lightly whisk. Heat the olive oil and butter in a large frying pan over a medium heat. Add the chopped chillies and cook for about 5–10 minutes, or until soft, being sure not to let them go brown. Add some sea salt and plenty of freshly ground black pepper and stir well.

Pour the eggs over the chillies and gently move the chillies around the pan, so you are literally folding the chillies through the eggs, until the eggs have started to set but are still a little bit runny. Be careful not to overcook the eggs, or they will be rubbery.

Serve immediately, with crusty bread.

SERVES 4

I make this dish when I feel like something a little fresh to go with my eggs. It's good in the morning, or the afternoon; you make up your own mind ...

This recipe can serve one person or two. Just vary the egg quantity accordingly, but keep the quantity of the other ingredients the same.

YUMURTA SALATASI

EGGS WITH TOMATO, RED ONION, CHILLI & PARSLEY

1 tomato, diced
1 tablespoon finely diced red onion
1 tablespoon finely chopped flat-leaf
   (Italian) parsley
1 long green chilli, finely chopped
2 free-range eggs per person
40 g (1½ oz) butter
crusty bread, to serve

In a small bowl, mix together the tomato, onion, parsley, chilli and some sea salt and freshly ground black pepper.

In another bowl, whisk the eggs with a pinch of sea salt.

Melt the butter in a frying pan over a high heat. Pour the eggs into the pan. Gently move the eggs around the pan with a wooden spoon, to make smooth chunks of egg, being careful not to overcook them.

When the eggs are cooked to your liking, spoon them onto a serving plate. Top with the tomato salad and serve warm, with crusty bread.

SERVES 1–2

For Turks, bread is the most important thing in life. Fresh every morning, noon and night, three times a day.

I love these straight out of the oven, with some cream cheese and a cup of black tea. In Turkey, just about every street corner will have a vendor selling *simits* and shouting, *'Simitçi! Simitçi!'*

SIMIT

SIMIT

600 g (1 lb 5 oz/4 cups) plain (all-purpose) flour
7 g (¼ oz/2 teaspoons) dried yeast
pinch of sea salt
pinch of sugar
375 ml (12½ fl oz/1½ cups) warm water, approximately
270 g (9½ oz/1¾ cups) sesame seeds
125 ml (4 fl oz/½ cup) pekmez (grape molasses; see note)

Put the flour in a large bowl and make a well in the centre. Sprinkle the yeast, salt and sugar into the well. Pour in 190 ml (6½ fl oz/¾ cup) of the warm water and stir from the centre, gradually drawing the flour into the dough; you will probably need to add the remaining warm water as you go.

Turn the dough out onto a floured surface and knead until it feels like your earlobe, about 10 minutes. Place in a bowl, cover and set aside to rise in a warm place until it doubles in size; this should take about 1 hour.

If you have a wood-fired oven, this is the time to light your fire. Otherwise, preheat your oven to 200°C (400°F). Line three or four baking trays with baking paper.

Punch the dough down lightly, then portion into walnut-sized pieces. Form each one into a bagel shape by making a hole in the middle and using your finger to widen out the hole — or you can roll each portion into a thin cigar and pinch the two ends together, into a bagel shape.

Sprinkle the sesame seeds onto a tray. Brush each simit with the pekmez and coat well on both sides with sesame seeds. The simit will stretch and will end up with a diameter of about 12 cm (4¾ inches). Place on another tray and allow to rest for 15–20 minutes, until risen slightly.

Now bake in the wood-fired oven — or, if you are using a domestic oven, spray a little water onto the simits to create some steam to make them crusty. Bake for 15 minutes, or until golden brown.

These are best enjoyed the same day.

MAKES ABOUT 20

NOTE

Pekmez is a thick, sweet, dark purple syrup, similar in consistency to molasses, made by boiling down the juice of crushed grapes. You'll find it in Middle Eastern grocery stores.

How gorgeous can you get? *Simitçi, Simitçi!*

My favourite bakery, called the Taş Fırın, in action, around the corner from my sister's house in Ankara.

This is all you need.

Five holy nights each year, the mosques throughout Turkey are all lit up brightly and special prayers are made. Each of these holy evenings are known as *Kandil* (meaning 'candle'). For these special religious celebrations, you buy or make these little babies to share with your loved ones.

KANDİL SİMİT

SESAME RINGS

1 free-range egg yolk, lightly beaten,
    for brushing
50 g (1¾ oz/⅓ cup) sesame seeds,
    for sprinkling
250 g (9 oz) unsalted butter,
    at room temperature
60 ml (2 fl oz/¼ cup) milk
60 ml (2 fl oz/¼ cup) olive oil
1 tablespoon mahlab (see note)
2 tablespoons caster
    (superfine) sugar
pinch of sea salt
300 g (10½ oz/2 cups) plain
    (all-purpose) flour

Preheat the oven to 180°C (350°F).

Set aside the egg yolk and sesame seeds. Put all the other ingredients in a large bowl and mix together to make a dough (using your hands is easiest). Allow to rest for about 10–15 minutes.

Divide the dough into 12 equal pieces, then roll each piece into a cigar, about 10 cm (4 inches) long, and 2.5 cm (1 inch) in diameter. Form each cigar into a circle by joining the two ends and pinching them together, making a bagel shape. Brush each circle with the egg yolk and sprinkle with the sesame seeds.

Place on a baking tray and bake for 30 minutes, or until golden brown. Enjoy warm, fresh from the oven.

MAKES 12

NOTE

Mahlab (also labelled mahaleb, mahlep, mahleb or St Lucie kernels) is a fragrant spice powder ground from the small seeds inside the pits of the wild, sour mahaleb cherry. You'll find it in spice emporiums and Middle Eastern grocery stores.

I love these babies. My favourite with a cup of tea, a little cheese ... I'm in heaven.

This is the Turkish version of brioche. It is amazing straight from the oven, and fantastic toasted with jam for breakfast. In my family I was the only one who made these. I love the aroma of the *mahlab* spice, which is ground from the seeds of wild black cherries; it smells like heaven, warm and sweet.

PASKALYA
SWEET BREAD

7 g (¼ oz/2 teaspoons) dried yeast
115 g (4 oz/½ cup) caster
    (superfine) sugar
180 ml (6 fl oz) milk, approximately,
    at room temperature
375 g (13 oz/2½ cups) plain
    (all-purpose) flour
1 tablespoon mahlab
    (see note, page 36)
120 g (4½ oz) unsalted
    butter, softened
2 free-range eggs, lightly beaten
1 free-range egg yolk, lightly beaten,
    for brushing
30 g (1 oz/¼ cup) slivered almonds

Preheat the oven to 180°C (350°F).

Mix the yeast, 1 tablespoon of the sugar and 60 ml (2 fl oz/¼ cup) of the milk in a bowl. Leave for 5–10 minutes, until the yeast turns frothy and 'comes alive'.

Combine the flour, mahlab and remaining sugar in a large bowl. Make a well in the centre and add the butter, beaten eggs, activated yeast mixture and most of the milk. Combine the mixture with your hands, adding a little more milk if needed to bring it all together into a dough.

Turn out onto a lightly floured surface and knead until the dough feels like your earlobe, about 10–15 minutes. Cover the dough and allow to rest in a warm spot until it has doubled in size, usually 2–3 hours.

Gently punch down the dough, then divide into three equal pieces. Roll each piece into a cylinder about 40 cm (16 inches) long, then braid the three pieces together, like you would plait your hair. Tuck the ends under neatly. Place on a baking tray and set aside for a further 20–30 minutes, until slightly risen.

Brush with the egg yolk and sprinkle with the slivered almonds. Bake for 30–40 minutes, until the bread is golden brown. Serve warm.

Any leftover bread will keep for a few days, wrapped in plastic wrap, and makes a wonderful bread and butter pudding.

MAKES 1 LOAF

When we were kids, Mum would get up really early in the morning and go to our neighbour's *tandır* — a special wood-fired brick oven, built into a pit in the ground. She would make these beautiful flaky breads, and then we'd all sit together and have them for breakfast. Whenever she knows I am coming home from Australia to visit her, she gets so excited she makes these breads four days ahead! But I do love them when she makes them on the same day — that's our little secret, sssh.

This bread is amazing when it's cooked on the flat plate of your barbecue or in a wood-fired oven. You will love the result. It is wonderful for breakfast with strawberry jam and Bulgarian feta, or honey and tahini, or anything savoury that your heart desires.

KATMER

FLAKY PASTRY BREADS

525 g (1 lb 3 oz/3½ cups) plain
  (all-purpose) flour
1 teaspoon sea salt
375 ml (12½ fl oz/1½ cups) milk
150 g (5½ oz) butter, softened

In a large bowl, mix the flour, salt and milk together, using your hands. Knead in the bowl for 10–15 minutes, to make a soft dough. Cover and leave to rest for 10 minutes.

Shape the dough into six balls, about the size of tennis balls. Flatten each ball with a rolling pin, then roll out into very thin circles about 1 mm (¹⁄₁₆ inch) thick.

Rub some softened butter into the surface of each round of dough. Working with one piece at a time, roll each round of dough up, into a long cigar shape, then twist it around itself, to make a snail shape.

Taking one snail at a time, flatten each one with a rolling pin on a floured surface so it's about 20 cm (8 inches) in diameter; it will be less than 5 mm (¼ inch) thick.

Heat a large non-stick frying pan over a medium–low heat. Cook the pastries in batches for 3–4 minutes each side, or until golden brown. Serve warm.

MAKES 6

DÜĞME KURABİYE

LITTLE BUTTONS

250 g (9 oz) unsalted butter,
   softened, plus extra for greasing
450 g (1 lb/3 cups) plain
   (all-purpose) flour
125 g (4½ oz/1 cup) icing
   (confectioners') sugar
140 g (5 oz/1 cup) hazelnuts,
   roasted, skinned and finely
   chopped (see note)

FOR THE TOPPING

3 tablespoons icing sugar
1 tablespoon ground cinnamon

Preheat the oven to 170°C (340°F). Grease a large baking tray with softened butter.

Place the 250 g (9 oz) butter in a large bowl and mix well with the flour and icing sugar. Fold the hazelnuts through.

Take small pieces of the dough and shape them into buttons about the diameter of a walnut. Place on the baking tray and bake for 10–15 minutes, or until golden.

Allow to cool, then sift the icing sugar and cinnamon over the top.

Your little buttons will keep in an airtight container in the pantry for 2–3 days.

MAKES ABOUT 40

NOTE

To roast hazelnuts, spread them on a baking tray and bake in a preheated 200°C (400°F) oven for 10 minutes, or until the skins have started to split, keeping careful watch that they don't burn. Remove from the oven and allow to cool slightly, then tip the hazelnuts into a sieve and shake the skins loose, or tip them into a clean cloth and rub the skins off. You can then finely chop them using a food processor.

In Turkey, many bakers use vanilla sugar, which you can buy in little sachets in any supermarket, but I love to make my own. Whenever I scrape the seeds out of vanilla beans, I just put the empty vanilla pod into a jar of sugar, which gives the sugar a lovely vanilla flavour.

FISTIKLI KURABİYE

PISTACHIO COOKIES

450 g (1 lb/3 cups) self-raising flour
185 g (6½ oz/1½ cups) icing (confectioners') sugar
60 g (2 oz) unsalted butter, softened, plus extra for greasing
125 ml (4 fl oz/½ cup) olive oil
100 g (3½ oz/1 cup) finely ground pistachio nuts
1 vanilla bean, split lengthways, seeds scraped
2 free-range eggs

FOR THE TOPPING

1 pistachio nut per cookie
sifted icing sugar, for dusting (optional)

Preheat the oven to 170°C (340°F). Grease a large baking tray with softened butter.

Put the flour in a large bowl and make a large well in the centre. Add all the remaining cookie ingredients to the middle of the well and mix them with your fingers, without bringing the flour into the middle.

Now gently start to bring the flour into the mixture, until a dough forms. Knead the dough for about 10 minutes, until it feels like your earlobe.

Break off pieces and form into round balls, about 2 cm (¾ inch) in diameter. Poke a pistachio on top of each cookie and place on the baking tray.

Bake for 25 minutes, or until golden. Allow to cool, then dust with icing sugar if desired.

The cookies will keep in an airtight container in the pantry for 2–3 days.

MAKES ABOUT 40

When I was a little girl, about eight or nine years old, I used to love making little biscuits when my mum was out of the house. I would get a bowl, put in some flour, the zest of a few oranges, a few tablespoons of yoghurt, some eggs, sugar and butter, then knead it all together and roll it into little balls. Worried that my cookies would get too big, I'd spread them out over eight or nine trays and bake them all up.

I'd be so proud and excited when my mum came home and I could tell her I'd made these beautiful biscuits — they were so amazing! It wasn't until many years later that I found out my dear brother Murat had confessed to the rest of the family that my biscuits were inedible, but he'd asked them not to tell me this, otherwise I'd stop making them. Maybe some of those days I was so excited I forgot to put the sugar or the love into the biscuits.

You could say that for Turkish people, life revolves around their stomachs. All day is spent thinking about food! In our home, once breakfast was finished, the dishes would be cleared away and the ladies of the household would start thinking about what to make for lunch. Some Turkish dishes take a while to put together, so as soon as breakfast was over, it was time to go shopping at the *pazar*.

Every neighbourhood has its own markets, where you can buy the most amazing tomatoes, eggplants, beans and different chillies. The lady of the house would be the hunter and gatherer, while the man would work hard to earn a few dollars to pay the bills.

Around 1 pm, our table would be set with all the lunch dishes — a bowl of yoghurt, a large bowl of salad, pickles, all the hot and cold dishes. The whole family would eat together, and all the dishes would be shared. Everyone would help themselves, although Mum would often ask us kids what we'd like to eat and serve up the dishes to us first. And then we'd all eat, and chat, and laugh, and enjoy our food together, and this would go on for hours.

Then, after lunch, it was time to clean up the dishes again — and start thinking about and preparing dinner!

PİDE

TURKISH BREADS

8 g (¼ oz/2 slightly heaped
teaspoons) dried yeast
½ teaspoon sugar
500 ml (17 fl oz/2 cups) warm water
600 g (1 lb 5 oz/4 cups)
plain (all-purpose) flour
1 tablespoon sea salt
60 ml (2 fl oz/¼ cup) olive oil,
plus extra for greasing
2 free-range eggs, lightly beaten
40 g (1½ oz/¼ cup) nigella seeds
(see note)
40 g (1½ oz/¼ cup) sesame seeds

Mix the yeast and sugar with 375 ml (12½ fl oz/1½ cups) of the warm water and set aside until the yeast starts foaming, about 5 minutes.

Combine the flour and salt in a large bowl. With your hands, gradually work in the yeast mixture, then mix in the olive oil and remaining warm water. Knead the dough until soft, about 10 minutes. Form into a large ball, rub with olive oil and place in a large bowl. Cover and leave in a warm place for 1 hour, or until doubled in size.

Preheat the oven to at least 250°C (500°F) and dust a few baking trays with flour. Divide the dough into 10 pieces. Take one piece of dough and roll it into a ball, then slightly flatten it. With wet hands, press and knead the dough into a rough circle. Stretch the dough out to a 25 cm (10 inch) circle, then brush with some of the beaten egg. Using the side of your hands, press out a border about 3 cm (1¼ inches) wide around the dough edge.

Dip your fingers into the beaten egg, point your fingers down to make a claw, and mark out four deep parallel rows in the dough without breaking through. Mark out another four rows, at right angles to the first four.

Sprinkle a wooden paddle or board with flour and lift the loaf onto it, stretching it out into an oval shape as you pull it onto the paddle. Brush well with more beaten egg and sprinkle some of the nigella and sesame seeds over the top. Repeat with the remaining dough to make 10 loaves.

Slide the dough onto the baking trays and bake for 8–10 minutes, or until golden. Wrap the loaves in a clean cloth and serve hot.

MAKES 10 SMALL LOAVES

NOTE

Nigella seeds look like tiny black sesame seeds. They have a unique aromatic flavour, and are often sprinkled over baked goods. You'll find them in spice shops.

This is my beautiful neighbour, who I grew up with. I've called her *teyze* — aunty — all my life.

KIYMALI PİDE

TURKISH PIZZAS

PIDE DOUGH

**525 g (1 lb 3 oz/3½ cups) plain
   (all-purpose) flour**
7 g (¼ oz/2 teaspoons) dried yeast
1 tablespoon sugar
2 tablespoons olive oil
**250 ml (8½ fl oz/1 cup) warm
   water, approximately**

LAMB TOPPING

250 g (9 oz) minced (ground) lamb
2 large onions, diced
2 vine-ripened tomatoes, finely diced
**1 tablespoon tomato paste
   (concentrated purée)**
**30 g (1 oz/1 cup) finely chopped
   flat-leaf (Italian) parsley**
4 long green chillies, finely diced
**1–2 tablespoons pul biber
   (see note, page 18)**
**1–2 tablespoons freshly ground
   black pepper**
1 tablespoon sea salt
50 g (1¾ oz) butter, melted

TO SERVE

lemon wedges
green leaf salad

To make the dough, put the flour in a large bowl. Add a pinch of sea salt and make a well in the centre. Mix the yeast, sugar, olive oil and 125 ml (4 fl oz/½ cup) of the warm water into the flour and start kneading the dough in the bowl. As you go, you can add some more warm water as needed. Knead for 10–15 minutes, until the gluten develops in the flour — the dough will be quite smooth and elastic and will feel like your earlobe.

Let the dough rest in a warm place away from any cool draughts for about 30 minutes, or until it doubles in size. Then punch it down and knead for a further 5 minutes. Portion into 12 pieces, place on a lightly floured tray and leave to rest for a further 10 minutes.

To make the topping, mix the lamb, onion, tomato, tomato paste, parsley, chilli, pul biber, pepper and salt together in a large bowl. Cover and marinate in the refrigerator for 2 hours, or overnight if possible; the mixture will be extra tasty if made the night before.

Working with one portion of dough at a time, thinly roll each one out into a boat shape or elongated oval, measuring about 20 × 30 cm (8 × 12 inches), and only about 2 mm (1/12 inch) thick.

Preheat the oven — or a pizza oven, if you are lucky enough to have one, as they give a beautiful result! — to 230°C (445°F). Place two pizza trays in the oven while it is heating up.

When the oven is hot enough, place the ovals of dough on the pizza trays; you should be able to fit two per tray. Thinly spread about 4 tablespoons of the lamb filling over each piece of dough, leaving a 1.5 cm (⅝ inch) border. Fold the edges over and pinch the ends together.

Bake in batches until golden brown, about 8–10 minutes. Brush immediately with a little melted butter.

Serve warm, with lemon wedges and a green leaf salad.

MAKES 12

You can have all kinds of different fillings in these delicious Turkish delicacies ... simple spinach and onion, or minced (ground) lamb and tomatoes.

When my mum was staying with me in Australia, I came home from work one day and she had a big smile on her face. She had made *gözleme* (with parsley, onion and tomatoes) in a non-stick frying pan! I was so proud of my mum — she used to make these only in a *tandır* oven, but she had already adapted to my humble kitchen, and the *gözleme* were really delightful. When my friends tasted her little delicacies, they all demanded to have bread-making lessons. They couldn't speak Turkish and Mum couldn't speak English, but my friends had the best lesson of their lives.

Instead of brushing your *gözleme* with melted butter, you can pan-fry them in sunflower oil and they will puff up beautifully.

In Turkey, these *gözleme* would be served with sweet black tea, and a Turkish yoghurt drink called *ayran*.

ISPANAKLI GÖZLEME

BREAD STUFFED WITH SPINACH

60 ml (2 fl oz/¼ cup) olive oil
2 brown onions, finely diced
500 g (1 lb 2 oz) English spinach, washed, dried and finely chopped
1 tablespoon pul biber (see note, page 18)
1 batch of Pide dough (see page 53)
melted butter, for brushing
lemon wedges, to serve (optional)

Heat the olive oil in a frying pan over a medium heat, then fry the onion until soft, about 6–8 minutes. Add the spinach and pul biber and season with sea salt and freshly ground black pepper. Cook for 1–2 minutes; you just want the spinach to soften.

Divide the pide dough into 12 pieces. On a floured work surface, flatten each ball with a rolling pin until it is only about 2 mm (¹⁄₁₂ inch) thick.

Spoon enough spinach mixture onto each portion to cover one half of the dough, leaving a 2 cm (¾ inch) border around the edge. Fold the other half over, into a half-moon. Press the edges together.

Heat a large non-stick frying pan over a medium heat. Brush the top of each gözleme with melted butter. Working in batches, fry the gözleme, buttered side first, for 4–5 minutes on each side, until golden brown. Brush with more melted butter as you are cooking them.

Serve immediately, with lemon wedges for squeezing over if desired.

MAKES 12

KIYMALI GÖZLEME

BREAD STUFFED WITH LAMB

2 tablespoons olive oil
2 brown onions, diced
200 g (7 oz) minced (ground) lamb
2 teaspoons sea salt
2 tablespoons pul biber
   (see note, page 18)
30 g (1 oz/1 cup) finely chopped
   flat-leaf (Italian) parsley
1 batch of Pide dough (see page 53)
50 g (1¾ oz) butter, melted
lemon wedges, to serve (optional)

Heat the olive oil in a frying pan over a medium heat, then fry the onion until soft, about 5–6 minutes. Add the lamb and cook with the salt, pul biber, parsley and a good sprinkling of freshly ground black pepper for a few minutes, until the lamb is just cooked and has changed colour, breaking up any large lumps.

Divide the dough into 16 pieces. On a floured surface, flatten each ball with a rolling pin until it is only about 2 mm (¹⁄₁₂ inch) thick.

Spread about 2 tablespoons of the lamb mixture over one half of each portion of dough, leaving a 2 cm (¾ inch) border around the edge. Fold the other half over, into a half-moon. Press the edges together.

Heat a large non-stick frying pan over a medium heat. Brush the top of each gözleme with melted butter. Working in batches, fry the gözleme, buttered side first, for 4–5 minutes on each side, until golden brown. Brush with more melted butter as you are cooking them.

Serve immediately, with lemon wedges for squeezing over if desired.

MAKES 16

When I walked back into my old home I met this beautiful woman, making bread to feed her family.

This is the exact place where my *soba* was. Thirty years later, I walk in and the Turkish fire is still burning.

Turkish *peynir* is a white cheese that comes in many different forms. It can be soft or hard, medium-fat or no fat. Traditionally it is made from sheep's milk. When I came to Australia I missed it so much.

Out of all the feta cheeses available to me here, the Bulgarian is the closest and the best I've found. It's sharp, it's creamy, and has a beautiful flavour. I think the Bulgarians owe me for using so much of their feta — we have tons of it at work! If I have no feta in the fridge it makes me feel as though I have no food at all. I could live on a little feta, a little tomato, and some Turkish bread to go with it.

This *gözleme* combines my favourite foods.

PEYNİRLİ VE MAYDONOZLU GÖZLEME

BREAD STUFFED WITH FETA & PARSLEY

250 g (9 oz) Bulgarian feta
30 g (1 oz/1 cup) finely chopped
   flat-leaf (Italian) parsley
2 tablespoons pul biber
   (see note, page 18)
1 tablespoon freshly ground
   black pepper
1 batch of Pide dough
   (see page 53)
melted butter, for brushing

Crumble the feta into a bowl. Add the parsley, pul biber and pepper and mix together.

Divide the dough into 12 pieces. On a floured surface, flatten each ball with a rolling pin until it is only about 2 mm (1/12 inch) thick.

Spoon enough feta mixture onto each portion to cover one half of the dough, leaving a 2 cm (¾ inch) border around the edge. Fold the other half over, into a half-moon. Press the edges together.

Heat a large non-stick frying pan over a medium heat. Brush the top of each gözleme with melted butter. Working in batches, fry the gözleme, buttered side first, for 4–5 minutes on each side, until golden brown. Brush with more melted butter as you are cooking them.

Serve immediately.

MAKES 12

This is the new home for our family. I am with my beautiful sister, Güfer.

Turks love their pickles. They pickle little cucumbers, eggplants (aubergines), green tomatoes, baby green melons, whatever they can get their hands on. Pickles are always served in small bowls to accompany lunch or dinner. You never mix them on your plate with your food — just eat them from the little bowls.

If you prefer, you can replace half the green chillies in this pickle with mild sweet banana peppers.

SALATALIK VE BİBER TURŞUSU

PICKLED CUCUMBERS & GREEN CHILLIES

1 kg (2 lb 3 oz) baby cucumbers
1 kg (2 lb 3 oz) long green chillies
6 garlic cloves, peeled
10 flat-leaf (Italian) parsley sprigs
400 ml (13½ fl oz) white wine vinegar
2 tablespoons sea salt

For this recipe you'll need two 2 litre (68 fl oz/8 cup) jars. Sterilise your jars, lids and utensils by running them through the dishwasher, or boiling them in a deep saucepan of water, then leaving them to drain upside down until dry.

Meanwhile, rinse the cucumbers and chillies well, then dry thoroughly.

Prick all the cucumbers with a fork a few times. Layer the cucumbers and chillies in the jars, adding three garlic cloves to each. Push most of the parsley sprigs in between.

Pour half the vinegar into each jar. Sprinkle the salt over the top, then pour in enough water to cover. Put some more parsley on top and seal the lids closed.

Turn the jars a few times to mix the salt through and break up the air bubbles. Leave in a cool dark place for 3 weeks before using. The unopened pickles will keep in the pantry for 2–3 months.

MAKES ENOUGH TO FILL TWO 2 LITRE (68 FL OZ/8 CUP) JARS

Turks like their salad ingredients chopped into bite-sized pieces. Just a bowl of green salad all chopped up together, or a salad of red onion, tomato, cucumber and green peppers. They eat salads as a complement to meals all throughout the day — breakfast, lunch and dinner.

ROKA VE HAVUÇ SALATASI
ROCKET & CARROT SALAD

250 g (9 oz) bunch of rocket (arugula)
60 ml (2 fl oz/¼ cup) extra virgin olive oil
pinch of sea salt
juice of 1 lemon
1 small red onion, thinly sliced
2 small carrots, finely grated

Trim any tough stalks from the rocket, then wash the leaves and drain. Mix the olive oil, salt and lemon juice together and set aside.

Put the onion and carrot in a serving bowl. Finely chop the rocket and add to the bowl with the lemon dressing. Toss together and serve at room temperature, with fish, meat or chicken dishes as desired.

The more peppery the rocket, the happier your liver. And hey, with all the vitamin A in the carrots, your eyes will be happy too!

SERVES 2

In Turkey, when chickpeas start coming into season, you will see people selling bunches of freshly picked chickpeas. Turks love to snack on these by simply nibbling on the fresh pea, straight out of the kernel. The skin is salty, but when you bite into the middle it is all sweet, so you get the beautiful sweet and salty flavour in your mouth. You can also buy the chickpeas dry-roasted or sugar-coated.

This salad can be enjoyed for lunch or dinner, with soft cheese and good crusty bread.

KABAKLI NOHUT SALATASI

ZUCCHINI & CHICKPEA SALAD

80 ml (2½ fl oz/⅓ cup) olive oil
2 zucchini (courgettes), cut into bite-sized pieces
1 red capsicum (bell pepper), diced
175 g (6 oz/1 cup) cooked or tinned chickpeas
2 long green chillies, chopped
3 spring onions (scallions), thinly sliced, including the green tops
30 g (1 oz/½ cup) finely chopped dill
15 g (½ oz/½ cup) finely chopped flat-leaf (Italian) parsley
juice of 1 lemon

Heat the olive oil in a frying pan over a high heat. Fry the zucchini for 4–5 minutes, or until soft — if you can get the right high heat to turn your zucchini brown, you will get a deep, sweet flavour. Add the capsicum, then stir and cook for a few minutes. Remove from the heat and allow to cool slightly.

In a bowl, mix the remaining ingredients together. Add the zucchini and capsicum and season with sea salt and freshly ground black pepper. Fold through and serve.

SERVES 4

PATATES SALATASI

POTATO SALAD

4 large potatoes, about 1.2 kg (2 lb 10 oz) in total, scrubbed but not peeled
1 red onion, diced
juice of 1 lemon
60 ml (2 fl oz/¼ cup) extra virgin olive oil
2 tablespoons süzme or labneh (see note), or plain (Greek-style) yoghurt
2 tablespoons thickened (whipping) cream
15 g (½ oz/½ cup) finely chopped flat-leaf (Italian) parsley
10 g (¼ oz/½ cup) mint leaves
8–10 radishes, thinly sliced

Bring a large saucepan of water to the boil over a high heat. Add the whole potatoes and return to the boil, then reduce the heat to medium. Simmer for 20–25 minutes, or until the potatoes are tender when pierced with a skewer. Drain and cool slightly.

While the potatoes are still very warm, peel them and chop into cubes. Place in a large mixing bowl with the onion, lemon juice and olive oil. Season with sea salt and freshly ground black pepper and fold together gently. Place to one side and allow to rest.

In a separate large bowl, mix the süzme and cream together. Add the potato mixture and fold through gently. Place on a serving plate and scatter the parsley, mint and radish slices on top.

SERVES 6

NOTE

Süzme is a soft, creamy strained yoghurt cheese, also known as labneh. You'll find it in many delicatessens and good food stores.

Turkey is blessed with the finest, freshest vegetables, all year round.

My beautiful nephew, Volkan, with me in Ankara.

In Turkey you can get black, white and red radishes that make this dish full of colour. The black and white ones are large and we grate them; the small red ones we slice. With their crunchy textures, we just adore them, especially splashed with just a little lovely olive oil and lemon juice.

This salad is a wonderful way to enjoy beautiful fresh radishes, and also to use your leftover stale Turkish bread.

TURP VE TERE SALATASI

RADISH & WATERCRESS SALAD

500 g (1 lb 2 oz) bunch watercress
8–10 radishes, thinly sliced
pinch of dried basil
80 ml (2½ fl oz/⅓ cup) olive oil
1 garlic clove, smashed
½ loaf Turkish bread (see page 50),
    cut into cubes
60 ml (2 fl oz/¼ cup) extra virgin
    olive oil
juice of ½ lemon

Trim the tough stalks from the watercress, then wash the leaves and drain off the excess water. Place in a large salad bowl with the radish and basil and gently toss together.

Heat the olive oil in a large frying pan over a high heat. Throw the smashed garlic clove in, then the bread cubes. Making sure the garlic doesn't burn, toss the cubes, frying for a minute or two until golden. Take off the heat.

In a small bowl, whisk the extra virgin olive oil and lemon juice together.

Tip the bread cubes over the salad, then sprinkle with sea salt and freshly ground black pepper. Drizzle the lemon dressing over and serve.

SERVES 4

Serve this simple salad with crusty bread and barbecued sardines, or any other oily fish that your heart desires.

ROKA SALATASI

ROCKET SALAD

60 ml (2 fl oz/¼ cup) extra virgin
  olive oil
juice of 1 lemon
250 g (9 oz) bunch of rocket
  (arugula)
15 black olives
1 vine-ripened tomato, chopped
  or cut into wedges

Whisk the olive oil and lemon juice together.

Trim any tough stalks from the rocket. Wash the leaves and drain off the excess water, then dry thoroughly. Arrange the rocket on a plate, tearing up any larger leaves a little if desired.

Scatter the olives and tomato over the rocket. Sprinkle with a pinch of sea salt, drizzle the dressing over and serve.

SERVES 2

If you can buy them fresh — or even better, grow your own — you will love these black-eyed beans. This salad is enjoyed with lunch as well as dinner.

BÖRÜLCE SALATASI

BLACK-EYED BEAN SALAD

400 g (14 oz/2 cups) dried
   black-eyed beans
1 tablespoon sea salt
1 brown onion
60 ml (2 fl oz/¼ cup) extra virgin
   olive oil
2 vine-ripened tomatoes, chopped
4 spring onions (scallions), sliced
2 long green chillies, diced
15 g (½ oz/½ cup) finely chopped
   flat-leaf (Italian) parsley
2 tablespoons lemon juice

Soak the beans in plenty of cold water overnight.

The next day, strain the beans and place in a large saucepan. Cover with plenty of fresh cold water and add the salt. Peel the onion and place in the saucepan with the beans.

Bring to the boil over a high heat, then reduce the heat to medium–low. Simmer, uncovered, for about 20 minutes, or until the beans are tender — the cooking time will depend on how old your dried beans are. Remove and discard the onion.

Strain the beans and place in a serving bowl while still hot. Pour the olive oil over, add the remaining ingredients and mix well.

This salad is especially delicious served warm.

SERVES 8–10

Most likely you will have this salad at lunchtime, or when you have unexpected guests and you want to make something quick and tasty. It is delicious and every Turkish household will have their own version. Here is mine.

CEVİZLİ KISIR

BURGHUL SALAD

175 g (6 oz/1 cup) fine burghul
 (bulgur wheat)
250 ml (8½ fl oz/1 cup) boiling water
125 g (4½ oz/1 cup) roughly
 chopped walnuts
6 spring onions (scallions), thinly
 sliced, including the green tops
15 g (½ oz/½ cup) finely chopped
 flat-leaf (Italian) parsley
20 g (¾ oz/1 cup) mint leaves
80 g (2¾ oz/⅓ cup) Turkish red
 pepper paste (see note)
2 tablespoons extra virgin olive oil
juice of ½ lemon
2 tablespoons pul biber
 (see note, page 18)

TO SERVE
lemon wedges
baby cos (romaine) lettuce leaves

Put the burghul in a saucepan. Pour the boiling water over and cover the pan. Leave to sit for 15–20 minutes, or until the water is absorbed and the burghul is nice and fluffy.

Combine the remaining ingredients in a serving bowl. Add the burghul and mix well.

Serve with lemon wedges and baby cos lettuce leaves.

SERVES 4

NOTE

Turkish red pepper paste, or *biber salcasi*, is a thick, hot, spicy, dark red paste made from red capsicums (bell peppers) and chillies. You'll find it in Middle Eastern grocery stores.

We cannot live without these yummy things: lentils, rice, beans, burghul (bulgur) …

PİYAZ

HARICOT BEAN SALAD

150 g (5½ oz/¾ cup) dried
    haricot beans
1 tablespoon white wine vinegar
1 vine-ripened tomato, chopped
15 g (½ oz/½ cup) finely chopped
    flat-leaf (Italian) parsley
1 red onion, diced
2 long green chillies, thinly sliced
2 tablespoons extra virgin olive oil
handful of black olives

Soak the beans in plenty of cold water overnight.

The next day, rinse the beans and place in a saucepan. Cover with fresh water and bring to the boil, then reduce the heat to medium. Simmer until the beans are soft; this usually takes about 40 minutes, or up to 1 hour.

Drain the beans and place in a bowl. Pour the vinegar over the hot beans and stir through. Let the beans absorb the vinegar for a few minutes.

Add the tomato, parsley, onion, chilli and olive oil. Season with sea salt and freshly ground black pepper and mix well. Scatter the olives across the top and serve.

This salad is especially fantastic with fish dishes.

SERVES 4

This is my all-time favourite way to eat zucchini. This dish can be served for breakfast, lunch or dinner ... but if you have it for breakfast, it isn't served with garlic yoghurt, as it is here.

If you are having a barbecue, you can just throw the zucchini rounds straight onto the grill, then drizzle them with olive oil before smothering them with the tomato; the browner the zucchini, the better they will be.

The garlic yoghurt is wonderful with meat, chicken and vegetables and will keep in the fridge for up to 5 days.

YOĞURTLU KABAK TAVASI

FRIED ZUCCHINI WITH GARLIC YOGHURT

250 ml (8½ fl oz/1 cup) olive oil
1 kg (2 lb 3 oz) zucchini (courgettes),
    cut into 5 mm (¼ inch) rounds
2 tomatoes, diced
1 tablespoon sea salt
crusty bread, to serve

GARLIC YOGHURT

2 garlic cloves, peeled
1 tablespoon sea salt
500 g (1 lb 2 oz/2 cups) plain
    (Greek-style) yoghurt

To make the garlic yoghurt, crush the garlic cloves to a smooth paste using a mortar and pestle. Gently fold the garlic and salt through the yoghurt; don't stir too vigorously as you don't want the yoghurt to liquefy. Cover and refrigerate until required; the garlic yoghurt is best served cold, as it tends to get a little runny at room temperature.

Heat the olive oil in a large frying pan over a high heat. Working in batches, fry the zucchini for a few minutes on each side, or until nicely browned; you want to bring out all their flavour. Remove and drain on paper towel. Drain the excess oil from the pan into a heatproof container to use again later.

Add the tomato to the pan and sprinkle with the salt. Cook over a high heat for 3–5 minutes, or until the tomato is soft, giving it a good stir every now and then.

Place the fried zucchini on a plate. Pour the tomato over and drizzle with the garlic yoghurt. Serve warm, with crusty bread.

SERVES 4–6

Garlic is one of the most important ingredients in Turkish cooking.

In the old days, you only had vegetables within their season, but nowadays most vegetables are available pretty much all year round. To celebrate the summer harvest, this is the dish to enjoy for lunch or dinner, with crusty bread. This stew is particularly tasty cooked in a traditional clay pot.

YAZ TÜRLÜSÜ

SUMMER VEGETABLE STEW

3 vine-ripened tomatoes
500 g (1 lb 2 oz) green beans
2 zucchini (courgettes)
2 carrots
125 ml (4 fl oz/½ cup) olive oil
2 brown onions, diced
1 tablespoon caster (superfine) sugar
30 g (1 oz/1 cup) finely chopped
    flat-leaf (Italian) parsley
crusty bread, to serve

Use a sharp knife to cut a cross into the bottom of each tomato. Place the tomatoes in a heatproof bowl and cover with boiling water. Leave for 30 seconds, then transfer to cold water and peel the skin away from the cross. Roughly dice the tomatoes and set aside.

Top and tail the beans, removing any strings, then chop into bite-sized pieces. Quarter the zucchini lengthways and cut into 1 cm (½ inch) pieces. Peel the carrots, quarter lengthways, then cut into 1 cm (½ inch) pieces.

Heat the olive oil in a saucepan over a medium heat. Fry the onion for 6–8 minutes, or until soft. Add the beans, carrot, zucchini and tomato. Sprinkle with the sugar, season with sea salt and freshly ground black pepper and mix everything together.

Turn the heat down to low, then cover and cook slowly for about 30 minutes, until all the vegetables are tender.

Take off the heat, sprinkle with the parsley and serve with crusty bread.

SERVES 4

This dish is eaten for both lunch and dinner. It is delicious served hot, straight out of the pan, but is also good cold.

PEYNİRLİ PATLICAN

EGGPLANT WITH FETA

3 eggplants (aubergines)
1 free-range egg
300 g (10½ oz) Bulgarian feta
30 g (1 oz/1 cup) finely chopped
 flat-leaf (Italian) parsley
plain (all-purpose) flour, for dusting
sunflower oil, for shallow-frying

Peel strips of purple skin from the eggplants, so they look like striped pyjamas.

Crack the egg into a bowl and lightly beat. Crumble the feta over, add the parsley and mash together.

Slice the eggplants into thin rounds, a bit less than 5 mm (¼ inch) thick.

Spread the feta mixture over half the eggplant rounds, then sandwich the remaining eggplant rounds on top. Dust all over with flour.

Heat about 2.5 cm (1 inch) of sunflower oil in a heavy-based frying pan, over a medium–high heat. Working in batches, fry the eggplant parcels for 3–4 minutes on each side, until golden brown. Drain on paper towel to absorb the excess oil. Serve hot or cold.

SERVES 4

Turks love to eat eggplant in many, many ways, and this is just another way: dried. We rehydrate these and stuff them full of love.

Also known here as 'lady's fingers', and in Turkey as *bamya*, okra should only ever be eaten when they are small and delicate — like a lady's fingers! — which is when they are still tender. Preparing them in the following way is very easy and delicious.

These fritters are traditionally enjoyed for lunch or for dinner.

BAMYA KIZARTMASI

OKRA FRITTERS

500 g (1 lb 2 oz) okra (look for small ones, remember!)
1 free-range egg
125 ml (4 fl oz/½ cup) sparkling mineral water
35 g (1¼ oz/¼ cup) plain (all-purpose) flour
pinch of sea salt, plus extra for sprinkling
sunflower oil, for shallow-frying
lemon wedges, to serve

Wash the okra and dry thoroughly. In a bowl, mix the egg, mineral water, flour and salt together, into a smooth batter.

Heat about 2.5 cm (1 inch) of sunflower oil in a heavy-based frying pan, over a high heat. Working in batches, dip the whole okra into the batter, then fry for 4–5 minutes, or until golden all over, turning halfway through. Remove and drain on paper towel.

Sprinkle with sea salt and serve hot, with lemon wedges.

SERVES 6–8

The Bosphorus reflected, Istanbul.

These delicious morsels can be rolled and shaped a day ahead, and cooked just before serving. In Turkey they are not only served up at lunch, but also enjoyed at dinner, too.

CEVİZLİ MERCİMEK KÖFTESİ

LENTIL & WALNUT KOFTE

185 g (6½ oz/1 cup) brown
   or green lentils
1 carrot, grated
2 tablespoons plain
   (all-purpose) flour
1 tablespoon grated cheddar
30 g (1 oz/1 cup) finely chopped
   flat-leaf (Italian) parsley
1 free-range egg
60 g (2 oz/½ cup) chopped walnuts
2–3 tablespoons dry breadcrumbs
sunflower oil, for shallow-frying
20 g (¾ oz/1 cup) mint leaves
Garlic yoghurt (see page 82),
   to serve

Put the lentils in a saucepan, cover with cold water and add a pinch of sea salt. Bring to the boil, then leave to boil until tender — usually about 35–40 minutes. Drain well.

Transfer the lentils to a food processor. Add the carrot, flour, cheese, parsley and egg. Season with sea salt and freshly ground black pepper and process until well combined.

Scrape the mixture into a large bowl and add the walnuts. Mix well, then shape into walnut-sized balls. Roll them in the breadcrumbs, place on a tray and refrigerate for a couple of hours, until firm and well chilled.

When you are ready to eat, heat about 2.5 cm (1 inch) of sunflower oil in a heavy-based frying pan, over a high heat. Working in batches, fry the kofte in the oil for 3–4 minutes, until golden all over, turning halfway through. Remove and drain on paper towel.

Place on a serving plate and serve hot, garnished with the mint leaves, and with garlic yoghurt on the side.

MAKES ABOUT 25

A statue of President Atatürk. His name means 'Father of the Turks', and this is my favourite place in Ankara.

Enriched with feta, these fritters are absolutely delicious, and equally enjoyable for lunch or dinner.

KARNIBAHAR MÜCVERİ

CAULIFLOWER FRITTERS

1 cauliflower, about 1 kg (2 lb 3 oz), broken into florets
1 tablespoon vinegar
7 spring onions (scallions), finely chopped
2 tablespoons plain (all-purpose) flour
30 g (1 oz/½ cup) chopped dill
1 free-range egg
100 g (3½ oz) Bulgarian feta
sunflower oil, for shallow-frying

In a large saucepan, heat enough water to cover all the cauliflower. Add the vinegar and bring to the boil, then add the cauliflower florets. Cook at a gentle boil until the cauliflower is soft, about 8–10 minutes. Pour into a strainer and drain well.

Put the cauliflower in a large bowl and mash well. Add the spring onion, flour, dill and egg. Crumble the feta into the bowl and season with sea salt and freshly ground black pepper. Mix together, then shape into little balls, about the size of walnuts.

Heat about 2.5 cm (1 inch) of sunflower oil in a large heavy-based saucepan, over a high heat. Working in batches, fry the fritters for about 3–4 minutes, turning occasionally, until golden. Don't over-crowd the pan, or the oil will lose too much heat, and the fritters will fall apart in the oil.

Drain the fritters on paper towel. Serve hot.

SERVES 4–6

There are many ways to prepare these flowers. You can stuff or fry them, but this is the easiest and simplest way to enjoy them. In Turkey they are nibbled on at lunch as well as dinner.

KABAK ÇİÇEGİ KIZARTMASI

FRIED ZUCCHINI FLOWERS

1 free-range egg
pinch of sea salt
35 g (1¼ oz/¼ cup) plain
    (all-purpose) flour
125 ml (4 fl oz/½ cup) milk
sunflower oil, for shallow-frying
16 zucchini (courgette) flowers
    (see note)
60 g (2 oz/1 cup) finely chopped dill
Garlic yoghurt (see page 82),
    to serve

Put the egg, salt and flour in a large mixing bowl. Slowly whisk in the milk, to make a batter.

Heat about 2.5 cm (1 inch) of sunflower oil in a heavy-based frying pan, over a high heat.

Working in batches of three or four, dip the flowers into the batter and fry for 2–3 minutes, or until golden brown, turning halfway through. Remove and drain on paper towel.

Serve hot, sprinkled with the dill, with garlic yoghurt on the side.

SERVES 4

NOTE

Zucchini flowers are available from good greengrocers during spring and summer. If small, thin zucchini fruit are attached to the flowers, you may need to double the amount of batter to cover the zucchini as well.

This is your typical *bakkal*, selling everything you might want.

When cooking dried beans and chickpeas, it's worth preparing a much larger quantity than you actually need, given their lengthy soaking and cooking times. Once cooked, they will keep beautifully in an airtight container or zip-lock bags in the freezer for several months. Then you can just pull them out of the freezer whenever you need them, and use them in all kinds of dishes.

These braised chickpeas are a lovely complement to pilafs.

NOHUT YAHNİSİ

BRAISED CHICKPEAS

440 g (15½ oz/2 cups) dried
  chickpeas
750 ml (25½ fl oz/3 cups) water
  or chicken stock
125 ml (4 fl oz/½ cup) olive oil
2 onions, diced
2 tomatoes, diced
2 tablespoons tomato paste
  (concentrated purée)
Burghul pilaf (see page 143)
  or steamed white rice, to serve

Soak the chickpeas overnight in plenty of cold water.

The next day, rinse the chickpeas and place in a saucepan. Cover with the water or stock and bring to the boil, then reduce the heat and simmer for 1–1½ hours, or until soft.

Strain the chickpeas and rub the skins off. Set aside.

Heat the olive oil in a large saucepan over a medium heat, then fry the onion for 5–6 minutes, or until soft. Add the diced tomatoes and tomato paste and fry for a couple of minutes.

Now add the chickpeas. Season with sea salt and freshly ground black pepper and cook for about 10–15 minutes, to mix the flavours together and heat everything through.

Serve with burghul pilaf or steamed white rice.

SERVES 4

Every Turkish region has its own version of the kebab, varying slightly according to what ingredients are locally available and in season, and thereby varying a little in taste. The kebabs from Adana, a city in the south-east of Turkey near the Syrian border, are very popular and can be found all throughout Turkey.

Adana kebabı can be eaten for lunch or dinner, and aren't usually served with any other accompaniments.

ADANA KEBABI

KEBABS FROM ADANA

40 g (1½ oz) butter
1 tablespoon pul biber (see note, page 18)
1 kg (2 lb 3 oz) minced (ground) sheep or lamb
2 white onions, peeled and grated
1 tablespoon Turkish red pepper paste (see note, page 78)
½ loaf Turkish bread (see page 50), cut into strips
250 g (9 oz/1 cup) Garlic yoghurt (see page 82)
chopped flat-leaf (Italian) parsley, for sprinkling

Melt the butter in a small saucepan over a gentle heat. Stir in the pul biber. Warm until fragrant, then set to one side.

Put the meat, onion and pepper paste in a large bowl and season with sea salt and freshly ground black pepper. Using your bare hands, mix together for at least 20 minutes.

Meanwhile, if using wooden skewers, soak eight skewers in cold water for about 20 minutes so they don't scorch on the barbecue.

Roll the meat mixture into sausage shapes and spear onto your skewers.

Meanwhile, fire up your barbecue or grill (broiler) to high. Cook the kebabs on the barbecue grill bars or under the grill for 5–6 minutes, or until the meat is cooked to your liking. Remove from the heat and allow to rest for a few minutes.

Meanwhile, take a heavy-based frying pan and dry-fry the bread strips on both sides until golden.

Place the bread strips on a serving platter. Remove the meat from the skewers, directly onto the bread. Spoon the garlic yoghurt over, sprinkle with parsley, drizzle the spiced butter over everything and serve.

MAKES 8

Shopkeeper Ali Gök, in Ankara, sells the most amazing array of pulses and produce I've ever seen: white rice, pink rice, every kind of bean ...

... These garlic bulbs were being sold by his son, just across the road.

I'm here again buying fresh bread for my family. Things have not changed very much.

Serve these with lunch, or if you have the barbecue going, you can make these kebabs as part of your mixed barbecue.

CİĞER KEBABI

BARBECUED LAMB'S LIVER KEBABS

500 g (1 lb 2 oz) lamb's liver, skin removed, sliced 1 cm (½ inch) thick
2 white onions
50 g (1¾ oz) butter, melted
Red onion & sumac salad (see page 140), to serve
Turkish bread (see page 50), to serve

Put the livers in a bowl and place in the refrigerator for 2 hours to allow the blood to drain.

Remove the livers from the bowl and squeeze gently to release any remaining blood. Discard the blood and return the livers to the bowl.

Peel the onions and grate them into another bowl. Wrap the grated onion in a piece of muslin (cheesecloth), then squeeze the juice over the livers.

Fire up your barbecue and bring it to a high heat.

Put the liver slices over the flames, onto the barbecue grill. Brush generously with the melted butter and sprinkle with sea salt and freshly ground black pepper as you cook. Turn after a couple of minutes and cook until the meat is done to your preference; I prefer mine still slightly pink in the middle — deliciously tender and not too dry.

Alternatively, you could heat a large frying pan over a medium–high heat and cook the kebabs for 1–2 minutes on each side.

Sprinkle with extra cracked black pepper and serve immediately, with the salad and bread.

SERVES 4 AS A MEAL, OR 6–8 AS PART OF YOUR MIXED BARBECUE

This is a great dish if you are having a family gathering for lunch — or for dinner, any night of the week. It would be wonderful to cook this in a wood-fired oven.

TAVUKLU PATATES

POTATOES WITH CHICKEN

2 tablespoons olive oil

8 chicken thigh cutlets, on the bone, and with the skin on; about 1.6 kg (3½ lb) in total

3 tomatoes, grated, juice reserved, skin discarded

1 tablespoon tomato paste (concentrated purée)

4 garlic cloves, peeled

125 ml (4 fl oz/½ cup) chicken stock or water

4 small desiree potatoes, about 500 g (1 lb 2 oz) in total, peeled and quartered

4 long green chillies

chopped flat-leaf (Italian) parsley, to garnish

crusty bread, to serve

Rocket salad (see page 74), to serve

Preheat the oven to 160°C (320°F).

Heat the olive oil in a large frying pan over a medium–high heat. Sear the chicken cutlets on both sides for a few minutes, until nicely browned. Remove from the pan and set to one side.

Add the grated tomatoes and all their juice to the pan, along with the tomato paste and garlic cloves. Season with sea salt and freshly ground black pepper and stir for about 5 minutes. Add the stock or water and mix through.

Place the potatoes in a deep baking dish, then layer the chicken over the potatoes. Add the whole chillies, then cover with the tomato sauce.

Cover with foil and bake for 35–40 minutes, or until the potatoes are tender and the chicken is cooked through. Sprinkle with parsley and serve with crusty bread and rocket salad.

SERVES 4–6

Lunchtime in Istanbul ...

In Turkey, when you go shopping at the *pazar*, you will see many different varieties of beans. Each stallholder will sell his specialty — maybe little ones in their kernels, or my favourite, flat green beans. This is a truly delightful way to enjoy beans. If you have a guest who is vegetarian, simply leave out the lamb — the beans will be just as delicious.

For lunch, serve this dish with salad and crusty bread; for dinner it is great with Tomato and rice pilaf (see page 144).

ETLİ TAZE FASULYE

GREEN BEANS COOKED IN LAMB

1 kg (2 lb 3 oz) flat green beans
80 ml (2½ fl oz/⅓ cup) olive oil
2 brown onions, diced
250 g (9 oz) diced lamb
2 tablespoons tomato paste
   (concentrated purée)
2 large tomatoes, diced

Top and tail the beans, removing any strings, then chop the beans into 2 cm (¾ inch) lengths.

Heat the olive oil in a large heavy-based saucepan over a medium heat, then fry the onion for 6–8 minutes, until soft. Add the lamb and cook until browned all over.

Add the tomato paste, then the beans, and stir. Add the diced tomatoes and season with sea salt and freshly ground black pepper. Cover and cook over a low heat for 15–20 minutes, or until the lamb is tender. During this time, make sure there are enough juices in the pan; if not, add a splash of water.

Serve warm.

SERVES 4–6

A deliciously simple lunch, this dish is fantastic eaten hot or cold, and is so good that no one will complain if you decide to serve it for dinner! If you like, serve a small bowl of long green chillies on the side, for extra fire and crunch.

ETLİ MAKARNA

PASTA WITH LAMB, TOMATO & GARLIC YOGHURT

140 ml (4½ fl oz) olive oil
155 g (5½ oz/1 cup) finely chopped onion
2 long green chillies, finely diced
200 g (7 oz) vine-ripened tomatoes, finely diced
2 tablespoons tomato paste (concentrated purée)
200 g (7 oz) minced (ground) lamb
30 g (1 oz/1 cup) finely chopped flat-leaf (Italian) parsley
2 tablespoons pul biber (see note, page 18)
500 g (1 lb 2 oz) bow pasta
Garlic yoghurt (see page 82), to serve
torn mint leaves, to garnish

Heat 60 ml (2 fl oz/¼ cup) of the olive oil in a heavy-based frying pan over a medium heat. Fry the onion for 6–8 minutes, or until soft.

Add the chilli, tomato, tomato paste and lamb and season with sea salt and freshly ground black pepper. Add the parsley and cook for a few minutes, until the lamb is cooked through. Stir in the pul biber, then remove from the heat and allow to rest while cooking the pasta. Reheat the tomato sauce for a few minutes just before serving.

Add the pasta to a large saucepan of boiling water and cook according to the packet instructions. Drain, then return to the pan and toss with the remaining 80 ml (2½ fl oz/⅓ cup) olive oil.

Divide the hot pasta among serving bowls. Spoon the tomato sauce over, then add a good dollop of garlic yoghurt to each bowl. Garnish with mint leaves and serve.

SERVES 4

In Australia I can get these babies straight off the trawler. Even if I live on the other side of the world, some things don't change.

When you're in Turkey and you see a restaurant sign saying *balıkçı*, please do go in because you will be in for a treat. Inside they will be frying up fresh anchovies from the Black Sea, or sardines, and they will serve these up in crusty bread with some beautiful salad for your delight.

In Turkey, this simple dish is enjoyed both for lunch and for dinner.

LİMONLU SARDALYA

CURED SARDINES

12 fresh sardines
2 garlic cloves, finely chopped
1 teaspoon freshly ground black pepper
juice of 2 lemons
extra virgin olive oil, for drizzling
finely chopped dill or flat-leaf (Italian) parsley, to serve
crusty bread, to serve

Clean the sardines by gutting them and removing the head. Gently pull the backbone away, so that you have a butterflied sardine in your hand. Rinse under cold water, then dry thoroughly with paper towel.

Lay the sardines flat on a flat glass tray (or other non-reactive tray), with the skin side down. Sprinkle generously with sea salt, then sprinkle the garlic over the fish, then the pepper. Drizzle with the lemon juice, covering all the fish. Cover and leave to cure in the refrigerator for 24 hours.

To serve, remove the fish from the tray and arrange on a serving plate. Drizzle with extra virgin olive oil and sprinkle with dill or parsley.

Serve immediately, with crusty bread.

SERVES 3–4

Turks don't usually drink during the day over lunch.
Of course, there is generally an exception to every rule.
This one is guaranteed to light your fire.

RAKILI KARİDES

PRAWNS COOKED WITH RAKI

500 g (1 lb 2 oz) raw headless prawns
   (shrimp)
60 ml (2 fl oz/¼ cup) olive oil
125 ml (4 fl oz/½ cup) rakı (see note,
   page 162)
pul biber (see note, page 18),
   for sprinkling
lemon wedges, to serve
Shepherd salad (see page 139)
   or green salad, to serve
bread, to serve

Peel and devein the prawns, leaving the tails intact. Place in a bowl, toss with the olive oil and a sprinkling of sea salt, and set aside.

Fire up your barbecue to a medium heat. Warm the rakı in a small saucepan, without boiling it.

Cook the prawns on the heated barbecue for 1–2 minutes on each side, or until just pink. Be careful not to overcook them, as they will keep cooking when you take them off the heat.

Arrange the prawns on a serving plate. Pour the warm rakı over and light the alcohol, using a twist of paper or a lighter — but don't use matches because they will spoil the flavour.

Serve hot, sprinkled with pul biber, with lemon wedges, salad and your favourite bread on the side.

SERVES 4

Two proud Turks in action, selling tea in Istanbul.

These flavoursome babies can be enjoyed for either lunch or dinner, with crusty bread.

MİDYE PİLAKİSİ

BRAISED MUSSELS

3 dozen mussels
80 ml (2½ fl oz/⅓ cup) olive oil
1 brown onion, diced
1 carrot, diced
1 small celeriac, peeled and diced
1 potato, peeled and diced
½ teaspoon caster (superfine) sugar
1 tomato, diced
1 long green chilli, chopped
1 tablespoon plain (all-purpose) flour
15 g (½ oz/½ cup) finely chopped
    flat-leaf (Italian) parsley
crusty bread, to serve

Scrub the mussels and remove any hairy beards. Rinse the mussels in cold fresh water, then leave to drain in a colander. Choose a large saucepan (with a lid) that is big enough to hold all the mussels.

Heat the olive oil in the saucepan over a medium heat. Cook the onion for 6–8 minutes, or until soft. Add the carrot, celeriac and potato and fry for 3–4 minutes.

Now stir in the sugar and season with sea salt and freshly ground black pepper. Cook for 10–15 minutes, until all the vegetables are soft.

Stir in the tomato, chilli and flour, then cook for about 2 minutes, stirring occasionally to ensure the mixture doesn't catch on the bottom of the pan. Add the mussels and mix them through. Cook for 2–3 minutes, then add the parsley.

Turn off the heat, cover the pan, then shake the pan a couple of times to open the mussels. Allow to rest for 5 minutes, discarding any mussels that haven't opened.

Serve hot or cold, with crusty bread.

SERVES 6

This recipe is best made with fresh anchovies, but if you can't get them, use fresh sardines, or any other small, oily fish you like. It's good to use an inexpensive portable fish grill basket (the type sold in camping and barbecue stores) to cook the anchovies in; the grill basket stops the delicate anchovies falling apart or slipping through the barbecue grill bars, and also makes them much easier to turn.

This dish is delicious with the Haricot bean salad on page 81.

BALIK KÜLBASTISI

BARBECUED FRESH ANCHOVIES

1 kg (2 lb 3 oz) fresh anchovies
125 ml (4 fl oz/½ cup) olive oil
juice of 1 lemon
lemon wedges, to serve
crusty bread, to serve

Clean and gut the anchovies. Rinse in cold water, pat dry with paper towel, then place in a bowl. Sprinkle generously with sea salt, drizzle with the olive oil and gently toss to coat.

Fire up your barbecue and bring it to a medium heat. Lightly oil a fish grill basket. Lay the anchovies on the bottom half of the grill basket, close the lid and fasten securely. (Depending on the size of your grill basket, you may need to cook the fish in batches.)

Place the grill basket across the barbecue grill bars and cook the fish for 1–2 minutes on each side, or until just cooked through.

Arrange on a serving plate and drizzle with the lemon juice. Serve with lemon wedges and crusty bread.

SERVES 4

NIGHT

DINNER & MEZE

When we were kids, Mum and Dad would take us to visit our grandparents in the village. Back then there was no electricity — the only light at night came from cooking fires or gasoline lamps.

Outside it would be so dark at night — pitch black — that as kids we would be scared to use the toilet, which was outside the house.

Years later my grandfather said that he'd come into the world too early. He wished he had been born at a later time, when the bright lights of electricity were shining above his head.

In those days my grandmother collected all the dried cow pats she could find and used them as fuel for her fire. She was a very sustainable cook, without even knowing it. Maybe this is how I got my passion for being a self-sufficient little Turk!

For dinner, once again, all the different hot and cold dishes would be laid out together on the table (or on a mat on the floor, back in the old days).

And the feasting and sharing and talking and laughing would begin all over again.

There are loads of different Turkish red lentil recipes, and this is just one of them. If you are driving through the night and you stop at a roadhouse, you will see many people eating this soup before the main course. Sometimes they eat it for breakfast as a cure for hangovers.

SÜTLÜ MERCİMEK ÇORBASI

RED LENTIL SOUP WITH MILK

80 ml (2½ fl oz/⅓ cup) olive oil
1 large onion, diced
1 tablespoon plain (all-purpose) flour
1 tablespoon tomato paste
  (concentrated purée)
125 g (4½ oz/½ cup) red lentils
1 tablespoon pul biber (see note,
  page 18), plus extra for sprinkling
250 ml (8½ fl oz/1 cup) milk

Heat the olive oil in quite a large saucepan. Fry the onion over a medium heat for 5–6 minutes, or until soft. Add the flour and tomato paste. Cook, stirring, for 5 minutes.

Now add the lentils, pul biber and 500 ml (17 fl oz/2 cups) water. Season with sea salt and freshly ground black pepper and bring to the boil, then reduce the heat and simmer for 20 minutes, or until the lentils are tender.

Stir in the milk and cook for a further 5 minutes, until heated through.

Serve as is, sprinkled with a little extra pul biber — or if you wish you can blend it to a smooth soup before serving.

SERVES 4

Christianity meets Islam in one happy house: *Ayasofya* (Hagia Sophia), Istanbul.

Soups are an essential food in Turkey, and can be consumed at all times of the day — maybe as a meal in their own right, or as part of a larger feast. Most Turkish homes would always start a meal with a bowl of soup. No matter how bare the cupboard, every Turkish woman can find something to make soup from.

In the summer we drink cold soup — perhaps a yoghurt and cucumber soup with a few herbs. In winter it could be another yoghurt soup, hot and tasty.

This is my favourite soup, and I will share my recipe with you.

YOĞURT ÇORBASI

YOGHURT SOUP

110 g (4 oz/½ cup) whole wheat
  (available from health food stores)
500 g (1 lb 2 oz/2 cups) plain
  (Greek-style) yoghurt
2 tablespoons plain (all-purpose)
  flour
pinch of sea salt
75 g (2¾ oz) butter
3 tablespoons dried mint

FOR SERVING

2 garlic cloves, mashed with
  a pinch of sea salt
crusty bread
4 spring onions (scallions), sliced

Put the wheat in a small saucepan and cover with water. Bring to the boil, then reduce the heat and simmer until soft, about 45 minutes. Strain and set aside.

In another saucepan, combine the yoghurt, flour, salt and 750 ml (25½ fl oz/3 cups) water. Whisk really well and place over a high heat, stirring constantly in the same direction until the mixture comes to the boil — if you don't do this, it will curdle. Once it boils, stop stirring and reduce the heat to low. Add the wheat to the soup, then simmer gently for 10–15 minutes, or until thickened.

Meanwhile, in a small frying pan, melt the butter over a low heat and add the dried mint. Fry for a few minutes, until fragrant.

Turn off the soup. Just before serving, stir in the mashed garlic. Pour the soup into individual serving bowls, then drizzle the mint butter over.

To eat, break off a bit of crusty bread, place some spring onion in the middle and take a bite, followed by a spoonful of soup. *Mmm mmm.*

On a hot summer's day, you can serve this soup chilled for lunch or dinner.

SERVES 4

When we were little kids and got sick, the first thing my mother did was make this soup. Simple and nourishing, this soup is equally enjoyable for dinner or lunch.

ŞEHRİYE ÇORBASI

TOMATO SOUP WITH LITTLE PASTA

3 large vine-ripened tomatoes
1½ tablespoons olive oil
1 tablespoon tomato paste
   (concentrated purée)
1 litre (34 fl oz/4 cups) chicken
   stock or water
110 g (4 oz/½ cup) rice-shaped pasta
   (known as *risoni* to the Italians,
   orzo to the Greeks and *şehriye*
   to the Turks!)
30 g (1 oz/1 cup) finely chopped
   flat-leaf (Italian) parsley
crusty bread, to serve

Put the tomatoes in a food processor and blend to a smooth purée. (You can peel the tomatoes first, if you wish, but I don't bother doing this.) Set aside.

In a saucepan, heat the olive oil over a medium heat. Add the tomato paste and fry for a few minutes, then add the tomato purée and cook for a few more minutes. Stir in the stock, then season with sea salt and freshly ground black pepper. Bring to the boil.

Stir in the pasta and parsley. Bring to a simmer and cook for 7–10 minutes, or until the pasta is tender.

Serve hot, with crusty bread.

SERVES 4

My favourite place in Ankara. Every season the *hal*, a big undercover market, rocks with freshness. Today we have okra, tomatoes, chillies ...

Turks love finishing some stews with lemon juice and eggs. They call this *terbiyeli*, which translates to 'well behaved'.

In Turkey, this soup is only ever eaten in the evenings.

BALIK ÇORBASI

FISH SOUP

1 kg (2 lb 3 oz) whole fish (a big fish, such as snapper, mulloway or mackerel), scaled and cleaned
1 large onion, finely diced
1 potato, finely chopped
1 carrot, finely chopped
1 celery stalk, finely chopped
3 bay leaves
2 free-range egg yolks
juice of 1 lemon
15 g (½ oz/½ cup) chopped flat-leaf (Italian) parsley
30 g (1 oz/½ cup) chopped dill

Put the fish in a stockpot, along with the onion, potato, carrot, celery and bay leaves. Pour in enough water to cover the fish. Bring to the boil over a high heat, then reduce the heat to low. Simmer for about 10 minutes, or until the fish flakes away from the bone at its thickest point, and the vegetables are tender.

Remove the fish from the stock, reserving the stock, and set aside until cool enough to handle. Discard the head, skin and bones from the fish. Gently flake the flesh and set aside.

Remove and discard the bay leaves from the stock. Strain the fish stock, reserving the stock and poached vegetables.

Put the reserved vegetables in a food processor, then pour in 1 litre (34 fl oz/4 cups) of the fish stock. Purée until smooth, then return to the stockpot and keep warm.

Mix the egg yolks and lemon juice together until smooth. Season with sea salt and freshly ground black pepper, then pour the mixture into the soup, stirring all the while. Heat, stirring, for 3–5 minutes, until the soup has thickened slightly.

Stir the poached fish through. Immediately remove from the heat. Serve sprinkled with the parsley and dill.

SERVES 4

This is a celebration soup. The stock is made from the parts of the animal that might otherwise be wasted — the head, the bones, the offal. The soup can be eaten for lunch or dinner ... depending on when you are getting married!

DÜĞÜN ÇORBASI

WEDDING SOUP

500 g (1 lb 2 oz) beef neck chops
1 tablespoon white wine vinegar
1 carrot, finely diced
1 large onion, finely diced
100 g (3½ oz) butter, melted
50 g (1¾ oz/⅓ cup) plain
   (all-purpose) flour
1 tablespoon Turkish red pepper
   paste (see note, page 78)
crusty bread, to serve

TERBIYELI

juice of ½ lemon
2 free-range egg yolks
125 ml (4 fl oz/½ cup) milk

Put the chops in a stockpot with the vinegar and 1.5 litres (51 fl oz/6 cups) water. Add the carrot and onion and bring to the boil over a high heat. Reduce the heat to medium and cook, uncovered, until the meat is falling off the bones, about 1½ hours. Take the stockpot off the heat and allow to cool.

When the meat is cool enough to handle, break it into bite-sized pieces and discard the bones. Strain and reserve the stock. You will need 1.25 litres (42 fl oz/5 cups) of stock; if there is not quite enough, top it up with water so you have the right quantity.

In a clean saucepan, melt the butter over medium heat, then add the flour and red pepper paste. Stir for a few minutes, to cook out the raw flour taste. Gradually stir the reserved meat stock into the flour mixture and bring up to a simmer.

For the terbiyeli, whisk the lemon juice, egg yolks and milk in a small bowl. Pour in 60 ml (2 fl oz/¼ cup) of the hot meat stock, mixing well. Season with sea salt and freshly ground black pepper, then pour this mixture back into the stockpot. Stir and add the meat pieces. Cook for a few more minutes, until the meat is heated through and the soup has thickened slightly.

Serve immediately, with crusty bread.

SERVES 4

At any wedding, any celebration, Turks will dance, anywhere — on the street or in an alleyway.

This eggplant dip can be eaten for lunch or dinner. It makes a great accompaniment to your barbecue or kebabs, or you can enjoy it all by itself with some good bread.

PATLICAN EZMESI
SMOKED EGGPLANT DIP

1 kg (2 lb 3 oz) eggplants
    (aubergines)
juice of 2 lemons
135 g (5 oz/½ cup) tahini
    (see note, page 197)
3 garlic cloves, crushed
1 tablespoon sea salt
125 ml (4 fl oz/½ cup) extra
    virgin olive oil, plus
    extra for drizzling
mint leaves, to garnish
pul biber (see note, page 18),
    for sprinkling

Poke four or five holes in each eggplant, using a sharp knife. Place the eggplant directly over the burner of a gas stove, or on a barbecue grill over a high heat. Turning the eggplants constantly with tongs, cook for about 10 minutes, or until they are soft around the neck.

Set aside until cool enough to handle, then peel off and discard the skin. Place the eggplants in a colander and let any bitter juices drain away for a few minutes.

Put the eggplants in a food processor with the lemon juice, tahini, garlic, salt and olive oil. Process until smooth.

Scoop into a bowl and rest in the refrigerator until required; the dip can be made a few hours or up to a day ahead, to let the flavours combine.

Just before serving, drizzle with a little extra olive oil, then garnish with mint leaves and a sprinkling of pul biber.

SERVES 4

When we were kids we'd run home from school, grab a bit of bread, wander into the garden and put some mint, parsley and spring onion (scallion) on our bread to have as a little snack — yum! This is a lovely salad to go with lamb cutlets or chicken.

NANE SALATASI

MINT SALAD

2 tomatoes, roughly chopped
½ red onion, thinly sliced
3 tablespoons sumac
   (see note, page 140)
1 teaspoon sea salt
2 tablespoons extra virgin olive oil
20 g (¾ oz/1 cup) mint leaves

In a bowl, mix the tomato, onion, sumac, salt and olive oil together.

When you are ready to serve, throw in the mint leaves and toss.

SERVES 2

Crossing thousands of years of history.

Served almost every day, this is one of the most favourite salads in every Turkish home. You will break a piece of bread, dip it into the juices, pop it straight into your mouth and life is good!

ÇOBAN SALATASI

SHEPHERD SALAD

500 g (1 lb 2 oz) vine-ripened
  tomatoes
2 Lebanese (short) cucumbers
1 red onion
2 long green chillies
30 g (1 oz/1 cup) chopped flat-leaf
  (Italian) parsley
100 ml (3½ fl oz) extra virgin olive oil
juice of 1 lemon
bread, to serve

Chop the tomatoes, cucumbers and onion into small bite-sized pieces and place in a large bowl. Thinly slice the chillies and add to the bowl.

Add the parsley, olive oil and lemon juice and toss to combine.

Season to taste with sea salt and freshly ground black pepper and serve with your favourite bread.

SERVES 4

When you have a kebab, or any barbecued meats, or Turkish pides, this is the salad to serve. It is so quick to prepare, so fresh in taste, and really complements the flavours of different meats.

SOGAN SALATASI

RED ONION & SUMAC SALAD

1 red onion, thinly sliced
15 g (½ oz/½ cup) finely chopped flat-leaf (Italian) parsley
2 tablespoons sumac (see note)
pinch of sea salt

This salad is best made just before serving. Just put all the ingredients in a bowl, rub together and serve!

If you don't like the smell of raw onion on your breath, you can rinse the onion slices before using them in the salad.

SERVES 2

NOTE

Sumac is a tiny reddish-purple berry that grows throughout the Middle East. The berries are dried, then crushed and added to dishes for a tangy, lemony zing. Ground sumac is available from spice shops and Middle Eastern grocery stores.

The view from my mother's house in Ankara.

Burghul, or *bulgur* as it is known to the Turks, is an essential part of the Turkish diet. It is available in two forms: *ince bulgur,* which is fine burghul for using in salads and *köfte* dishes, and *iri bulgur*, which is a coarser burghul used for pilafs.

BULGUR PİLAVI

BURGHUL PILAF

50 g (1¾ oz) butter
2 large white onions, finely chopped
60 g (2 oz/¼ cup) tomato paste
   (concentrated purée)
2 long green chillies, finely chopped
350 g (12½ oz/2 cups) coarse burghul
   (bulgur wheat)

Melt the butter in a heavy-based saucepan over a medium–low heat. Add the onion and cook until translucent, about 6–8 minutes. Stir in the tomato paste and chilli and season with sea salt and freshly ground black pepper. Cook for a few more minutes.

Add the burghul and cook for 3–4 minutes, stirring gently. Pour in 750 ml (25½ fl oz/3 cups) water, bring to the boil and stir. Cover, reduce the heat and simmer for 15–20 minutes, or until the burghul is tender.

Turn the heat off and allow the burghul to rest for 20–30 minutes. Stir again and serve.

SERVES 8–10

Turkish people love their pilafs. If you have this one for lunch, serve it with a simple salad. For dinner it will usually accompany some form of meat dish.

DOMATESLİ PİRİNÇ PİLAVI

TOMATO & RICE PILAF

2 tomatoes
50 g (1¾ oz) butter
1 tablespoon tomato paste
  (concentrated purée)
200 g (7 oz/1 cup) medium-
  grain white rice
250 ml (8½ fl oz/1 cup) vegetable
  or chicken stock, or water

Grate the tomatoes into a bowl. Discard the skins, but keep the juice; you should have about 250 g (9 oz/1 cup) grated tomatoes and juice.

Melt the butter in a heavy-based saucepan over a medium heat. Add the grated tomatoes, reserved tomato juice and the tomato paste and season with sea salt and freshly ground black pepper. Wash the rice and add to the tomato mixture, then cook for 3 minutes, gently stirring.

Add the stock, stir and bring to the boil. Reduce the heat to low and simmer until the juices have evaporated, about 12–14 minutes. Put the lid on and cook for a further few minutes, until the rice is just tender.

Remove from the heat and allow to rest with the lid on for 15–20 minutes. Stir gently and serve.

SERVES 4

Istanbul at sunset.

When we were kids, we used to call broad beans 'donkey beans', as *eşşek* means donkey in Turkish.

Here are your beautiful broad beans, starring in a pilaf that can be enjoyed with lunch or dinner. I love this with Garlic yoghurt (see page 82), or with grilled chicken or grilled fish. I just *love* it!

EŞŞEK BAKLASI PİLAVI

BROAD BEAN PILAF

50 g (1¾ oz) butter
1 large white onion, diced
200 g (7 oz/1 cup) long-grain white rice
375 ml (12½ fl oz/1½ cups) chicken stock or water
500 g (1 lb 2 oz) broad beans, double shelled (see note)
30 g (1 oz/½ cup) chopped dill

Melt the butter in a heavy-based saucepan over a medium–low heat. Add the onion and cook until translucent, about 6–8 minutes.

Turn the heat up to medium, then add the rice and cook for 5 minutes, constantly stirring. Season with sea salt and freshly ground black pepper.

Add the stock, then cover and cook over a low heat for 10 minutes. Now add the broad beans, stirring gently. Sprinkle the dill over the beans.

Place a clean tea towel (dish towel) over the saucepan, then put the lid on. Remove from the heat and allow the pilaf to rest for 30 minutes before serving.

SERVES 4–6

NOTE

To prepare fresh broad beans, remove the beans from their long, thick outer seed pods, then place the individual beans in the freezer for an hour or two. Remove the beans and allow to thaw, and it will then be easy to slip each bean from its thin outer skin. If you buy frozen beans, you only have to remove the thin skins around the individual beans.

I would eat this pilaf for lunch or dinner, with just a bowl of leafy greens and some chopped spring onions (scallions). It is lovely with chicken, but can be served with any meat dishes.

NUHUTLU PİLAV

CHICKPEA PILAF

110 g (4 oz/½ cup) dried chickpeas
60 ml (2 fl oz/¼ cup) olive oil
400 g (14 oz/2 cups) medium-grain white rice
750 ml (25½ fl oz/3 cups) vegetable or chicken stock, or water

Soak the chickpeas overnight in plenty of cold water.

The next day, rinse the chickpeas and place in a saucepan. Cover with fresh water and bring to the boil. Reduce the heat and simmer for 1–1½ hours, or until the chickpeas are soft.

Strain the chickpeas and rub off their skins. Set aside.

In a large saucepan, heat the olive oil over a medium heat. Add the rice and fry for a few minutes. Pour in the stock, season with sea salt and freshly ground black pepper and bring to the boil.

Add the chickpeas, then reduce the heat to low. Cover and simmer for 10 minutes. Remove from the heat.

Quickly lift the lid and place a clean tea towel (dish towel) over the saucepan. Replace the lid and set to one side. Allow the pilaf to rest for 30 minutes before serving.

SERVES 6–8

I can eat anything that comes from the *hal*. I love the energy, the food, the freshness. I have to take you there one day. Will you come?

In Turkey, you would most likely have this pilaf for dinner, but nothing should stop you from eating it for lunch!

I love this dish served with Braised chickpeas (see page 99) and green salad. I remember as a kid, my mum would serve this dish with Pickled cucumbers and green chillies (see page 63) and small raw onions, which we burst with the heel of our hand.

You put the pilaf on a serving tray and pile the chicken on top. Then you put the bowls of pickles and salad and braised chickpeas and smashed onions on the table and dine to your heart's content.

TAVUKLU PİLAV

CHICKEN PILAF

1 medium free-range, organic, well-loved chicken
1 tablespoon sea salt, plus extra for seasoning
60 ml (2 fl oz/¼ cup) olive oil
1 tablespoon pine nuts
1 onion, peeled and grated
400 g (14 oz/2 cups) medium-grain white rice
rocket (arugula) leaves, to garnish

Put the chicken in a large saucepan and cover with cold water. Add the 1 tablespoon salt and bring to the boil. Reduce the heat to medium, leave the lid off and poach the chicken for 30–40 minutes, or until it is cooked through; the juices should run clear when tested with a skewer through the thickest part of the thigh. Remove the chicken from the pan and put it to one side; reserve the chicken stock.

In another saucepan, heat the olive oil over a medium heat. Add the pine nuts and fry for a few minutes until golden, tossing the pan so they don't burn. Then add the onion and rice and fry together for a few minutes.

Pour in enough of the reserved chicken stock to just cover the rice. Season with extra salt and reduce the heat to low. Put the lid on and cook for about 20 minutes, until all the liquid is absorbed. Turn the heat off and let the pilaf rest with the lid on for 30 minutes before serving.

There are a couple of different ways I like to serve this dish. One is to cut the chicken into pieces and place it on top of the rice, just before you take it from the heat; sprinkle with a generous amount of freshly ground black pepper and replace the lid. Another way is to cut the chicken into pieces, pan-fry them in a little olive oil until golden, then serve with the pilaf on the side. Or you could remove the skin and bones from the poached chicken, shred the chicken and toss it through the pilaf.

Whichever way you choose, some rocket leaves make a pretty garnish.

SERVES 6

NOTE

To make a plain rice pilaf, omit the chicken and pine nuts, and have approximately 500 ml (17 fl oz/2 cups) of hot chicken stock handy, to pour over the rice.

In Turkey there are loads of different recipes for *köfte*. This is just one way of enjoying beautiful beef. Besides barbecuing the *köfte*, you could also pan-fry them in some olive oil, over a medium heat, until cooked through.

Another way to enjoy this dish is to thinly slice some eggplants (aubergines) lengthways, brush on both sides with olive oil and fry on both sides until golden. Sprinkle each eggplant slice with sea salt, place a *köfte* on top and roll it up. Yummm.

KURU KÖFTE

BEEF KOFTE

500 g (1 lb 2 oz) minced (ground) beef, not too lean (you need a medium level of fat)
3 slices stale bread, crusts removed
2 brown onions
2 garlic cloves, crushed
1 tablespoon cumin seeds, toasted and ground (see note, page 173)
1 tablespoon freshly ground black pepper
1 free-range egg, lightly whisked
30 g (1 oz/1 cup) finely chopped flat-leaf (Italian) parsley
60 ml (2 fl oz/¼ cup) olive oil
Shepherd salad (see page 139), to serve

Put the beef in a large bowl. Dampen the bread by quickly dipping each slice in water. Squeeze the water out and add the bread to the bowl. Add the remaining ingredients — except the salad, of course! — and mix together really well. (You can cook the kofte straight away, or cover and let the flavours develop in the refrigerator overnight.)

Light your fire, or fire up your barbecue to a medium–high heat.

Shape a little piece of beef into a sausage the size of your index finger. Cook one before you shape any more, to check if you need to adjust the seasoning. That's what I always do.

Now shape all the sausages and take them on a tray over to the fire or barbecue. Cook until they are done — this should only take 2–3 minutes on each side.

Serve hot, with shepherd salad.

SERVES 8

Whenever we need to build a fire or have a picnic, we must see this man first and buy some coal.

For this dish, be sure to use minced lamb with some fat in it. Don't panic, most of the fat will come out in the cooking, but it will make your *köfte* taste divine and not dry. The bicarbonate of soda may seem an unusual addition, but it binds the *köfte* together and gives them a beautiful texture.

These are fantastic for picnics or cocktail parties, any time of the day.

CIZBIZ KÖFTESI

SIZZLING KOFTE

500 g (1 lb 2 oz) minced (ground) lamb, with medium fat content
2 garlic cloves, crushed
1 large white onion, peeled and grated
50 g (1¾ oz/½ cup) dry breadcrumbs
1 tablespoon cumin seeds, toasted and ground (see note, page 173)
1 teaspoon bicarbonate of soda (baking soda)
olive oil, for brushing
Rocket salad (see page 74) or Shepherd salad (see page 139), to serve
grilled lemon wedges, to serve (optional)

Put the lamb, garlic, onion, breadcrumbs, cumin and bicarbonate of soda in a large bowl. Season with sea salt and freshly ground black pepper and mix together well. Cover and rest in the refrigerator for 30 minutes.

You can cook these babies on the barbecue, brushing them with olive oil, or in a large, lightly oiled, heavy-based frying pan.

Before you start making all your kofte, take a little piece of the lamb and shape it into a sausage the size of your index finger. Cook one before you shape any more, to check if you need to adjust the seasoning.

Have a little bowl of water next to you. Wet your hands and break the lamb mixture into walnut-sized pieces. Roll each piece into the shape of a little sausage, until you have shaped all your kofte.

Cook the kofte over a high heat for 2 minutes on each side, or until nicely browned and cooked through.

Serve hot or cold, with your choice of salad, and perhaps some lemon wedges that you have quickly grilled up with the kofte.

SERVES 8

Sunset over Galata Bridge, Istanbul. Even in a city of millions and millions and millions, you still have to feed your family ...

This dish is a labour of love, but amazingly delicious. When we make it at home, a few of us will get together, drink tea, gossip, drink more tea, and before we know it all the *manti* are made and cooked. Maybe you could invite some friends over and perhaps drink some wine — but not too much, or it will take twice as long!

Because this makes a large quantity, it is possible to freeze the dumplings before baking. Pull them out of the freezer before you leave for work and leave them to thaw; you can then come home after a hard day's work, pop them into the oven and bake as directed in the recipe. So easy.

MANTI

TRADITIONAL TURKISH BEEF DUMPLINGS, WITH GARLIC YOGHURT & PAPRIKA BUTTER

375 g (13 oz/2½ cups) plain
(all-purpose) flour
1 teaspoon sea salt
1 free-range egg, lightly whisked
80 ml (2½ fl oz/⅓ cup) cold water
60 ml (2 fl oz/¼ cup) olive oil, plus
extra for greasing
Garlic yoghurt (see page 82),
to serve

FILLING

200 g (7 oz) minced (ground) beef
1 brown onion, peeled and grated
2 tablespoons finely chopped
flat-leaf (Italian) parsley

PAPRIKA BUTTER

60 g (2 oz) butter
1 tablespoon sweet paprika

Sift the flour and salt into a bowl. Make a well in the centre, then add the egg, cold water and olive oil. Using your hands, mix together to make a dough. Turn out onto a floured surface and knead well for about 15 minutes, until the dough is elastic and soft, and feels like your earlobe.

Oil the bowl and return the dough to it. Cover with a damp cloth and allow to rest for 1 hour at room temperature.

Preheat the oven to 170°C (340°F). Put all the filling ingredients in a bowl, season with sea salt and freshly ground black pepper and mix together.

Turn the dough out onto a well-floured surface. Knead for 5 minutes, then divide into halves. Cover one half with a damp cloth while you work with the other half. Roll out the dough using a thin rolling pin. You want the dough to be as thin as possible — maybe as thick as two sheets of paper. Now cut into squares about 5 cm (2 inches) across.

Spoon a tiny teaspoon of filling onto each square. Lift each corner and pinch together, to create a little bow at the peak of the dumpling. Place each dumpling on a floured surface as you finish making the first batch, then use the second dough portion and the remaining filling to make as many of these delicious morsels as you can.

Place the dumplings in a well-oiled baking dish and bake for 20 minutes, or until the edges turn slightly brown. Remove from the oven, then pour 1 litre (34 fl oz/4 cups) boiling water over the dumplings. Cover with foil and bake for another 15–20 minutes, or until the water is absorbed and the dumplings are soft.

Meanwhile, make the paprika butter by gently melting the butter in a small saucepan and stirring the paprika through. Leave to infuse until needed.

Transfer the dumplings to serving plates and generously dollop with garlic yoghurt. Drizzle with the paprika butter and serve.

SERVES 10 GENEROUSLY

Istanbul's Grand Bazaar.

When I was growing up, meat was our favourite, even though we couldn't afford to buy too much of it. Turkey has four seasons, so of course we ate lamb in spring when they were born, sheep in summer, and mutton in winter.

I remember once we were at my grandmother's house and she made a sheep and eggplant (aubergine) stew. I was only a little girl, and I picked up a piece of sheep from the stew and it tasted so good. But I got busted! I can still feel my grandmother chasing me out of the kitchen.

KUŞBAŞI KEBABI

LAMB KEBABS

1 kg (2 lb 3 oz) lamb, diced into 2 cm (¾ inch) chunks
1 large white onion, peeled
½ teaspoon ground allspice
1 tablespoon plain (all-purpose) flour
250 ml (8½ fl oz/1 cup) beef stock
¼ teaspoon ground cumin
¼ teaspoon ground cinnamon
Burghul pilaf (see page 143), to serve

Put the lamb in a bowl. Grate the onion, wrap it up in a piece of muslin (cheesecloth) and squeeze the onion juices over the lamb. Add the allspice, season with sea salt and freshly ground black pepper and mix everything together with your bare hands. Cover and marinate in the refrigerator for 2–3 hours, or overnight if you have time.

Fire up your barbecue and bring it to a medium–high heat. If using wooden skewers, soak them in cold water for 20 minutes so they don't scorch on the barbecue.

Spear each piece of lamb onto your skewers, reserving the juices from the bowl. Cook the kebabs on the barbecue grill bars for 2 minutes, then turn them over and cook on the other side. Remove from the heat and allow the kebabs to rest for a few minutes.

While the kebabs are resting, put the flour, reserved juices and stock into a small saucepan and whisk briskly, then add the cumin and cinnamon. Put the pan over a high heat and bring to the boil.

Arrange the kebabs on a serving platter, pour the hot juices over and serve immediately, with burghul pilaf.

SERVES 6

This is a great way to have fire at your table. In Turkey we use small twists of paper to light the fire, but I am sure you can use a lighter. Do not use matches, as the smell will linger and spoil this delicacy.

This dish would be served as part of the *meze* or dinner.

ALEVLİ PASTIRMA

RAKI-FLAMED PASTRAMI

200 g (7 oz) sliced pastrami
60 ml (2 fl oz/¼ cup) raki (see note)

Arrange the pastrami slices on individual serving plates.

Warm the raki in a small saucepan over a low heat, without boiling. Carefully light the raki with a lighter or a twist of paper, then pour a good splash of the flaming raki over each serve of pastrami. Eat immediately.

If there's any raki left, just drink it!

SERVES 4

NOTE

Turkey's national drink, *rakı*, is a clear, fiery, unsweetened aniseed-flavoured brandy distilled from grapes, similar to Greek *ouzo*, Italian *grappa* and French *pastis*. It is often served with *meze* dishes and is especially good with seafood. Often it is mixed with a little water to dilute it, which turns the *rakı* milky white — when it is known as 'lion's milk', or the milk of the brave!

Everyone needs one of these shops in their neighbourhood.

Lighting my way home.

There is nothing quite like the taste of kebabs cooked on the grill bars of a barbecue, but if you don't have a barbecue, you can cook them under your oven grill (broiler), set to medium–high heat. Always allow your cooked kebabs to rest for a few minutes before serving, so they are as tender and juicy as can be.

DOMATESLİ VE BİBERLİ KUZU KEBABI

LAMB KEBABS WITH SPRING ONIONS

1 kg (2 lb 3 oz) lamb backstraps
   or loin fillets, cut into
   2 cm (¾ inch) cubes
1 large white onion, peeled
10 bay leaves
4 vine-ripened tomatoes
12 long green chillies
30 g (1 oz/1 cup) finely chopped
   flat-leaf (Italian) parsley
8 spring onions (scallions), chopped
Rice pilaf (see Chicken pilaf note on
   page 151), to serve
Shepherd salad (see page 139),
   to serve

Put the lamb in a bowl. Grate the onion, wrap it up in a piece of muslin (cheesecloth) and squeeze the onion juices over the lamb. Season with sea salt and freshly ground black pepper and mix together well. Cover and marinate in the refrigerator for 1 hour, or overnight if you have time.

Fire up your barbecue to a high heat. If using wooden skewers, soak them in cold water for 20 minutes so they don't scorch on the barbecue.

Thread a few cubes of lamb onto a skewer, then a bay leaf and more lamb, until the skewer is full. Repeat with the remaining lamb and bay leaves. Set aside.

Quarter the tomatoes. Now spear a piece of tomato onto a skewer, then a whole chilli, skewered along its length. Alternate to the end of the skewer, repeating with more skewers until all the tomato and chillies are used.

Cook the kebabs on the barbecue grill bars for 2 minutes, sprinkling with sea salt, then turn them over and cook on the other side to your heart's desire. Remove from the heat and allow the kebabs to rest for a few minutes.

Sprinkle with the parsley and spring onion. Serve on a bed of rice pilaf, with shepherd salad on the side.

SERVES 6

As with most meat dishes, you would have these kebabs for dinner, unless you are going on a picnic, when you would have them with salad.

YOĞURTLU ŞİŞ KEBAB

LAMB KEBABS WITH YOGHURT

1 kg (2 lb 3 oz) boned lamb shoulder, lightly trimmed of excess fat, then diced into 4 cm (1½ inch) cubes
3 white onions, peeled
½ teaspoon ground allspice
1 whole Turkish bread (see page 50), sliced into 3 cm (1¼ inch) widths
100 g (3½ oz) butter
250 ml (8½ fl oz/1 cup) beef stock
250 g (9 oz/1 cup) plain (Greek-style) yoghurt
1 tablespoon pul biber (see note, page 18)

Put the lamb in a stainless steel bowl. Grate the onions, wrap them up in a piece of muslin (cheesecloth) and squeeze the onion juices over the lamb. Add the allspice, season with sea salt and freshly ground black pepper, then mix together well. Cover and refrigerate until needed, or overnight if you have time.

Fire up your barbecue and bring it to a high heat. If using wooden skewers, soak them in cold water for 20 minutes so they don't scorch on the barbecue.

Skewer the cubes of lamb and cook on the barbecue grill bars for about 3 minutes on each side, or until done to your liking. Remove from the heat and leave to rest for a few minutes.

Warm the bread slices on the barbecue for a minute or so on each side, until slightly charred and crispy. Arrange on a serving plate.

Meanwhile, in a small saucepan, melt half the butter, then add the stock and bring to the boil. Sprinkle the charred bread with sea salt, then drizzle with the buttery stock mixture.

In another small saucepan, combine the remaining butter and pul biber and warm through.

Spoon the yoghurt over the lamb skewers and pour the warm spiced butter over the top. Serve immediately.

SERVES 6

Two proud Turks, working deep into the night.

HURMA KEBABI

BEEF KEBABS

1 kg (2 lb 3 oz) minced (ground)
beef, not too lean (you need a
medium level of fat)
2 white onions, diced quite finely
½ teaspoon ground cinnamon
2 tablespoons pul biber (see note,
page 18)
50 g (1¾ oz/1 cup) chopped mint
30 g (1 oz/1 cup) finely chopped
flat-leaf (Italian) parsley
Shepherd salad (see page 139),
to serve
crusty bread, to serve

You will need six flat metal skewers for this recipe.

Place the beef in a bowl and season with sea salt and freshly ground black pepper. Add the onion, cinnamon, pul biber, mint and parsley and mix really well with your bare hands. Please don't hold back. Think of all the beautiful things in your life, or perhaps think of someone you absolutely adore. The more love that goes into your food, the better. You'll need to mix for at least 15 minutes, or until the mixture is sticky.

Fire up your barbecue or grill (broiler) to a high heat. Form the beef along your metal skewers, into one long sausage shape per skewer.

Cook on the barbecue grill bars, or under the grill, for 3–4 minutes on each side, or until just cooked through. Remove the skewers from the kebabs and serve immediately, with shepherd salad and crusty bread.

SERVES 6

Bayram is the Turkish word for 'festival' and is always accompanied with great feasting. This dish is cooked to mark the end of two different Muslim holy periods: Ramadan (or *Ramazan* as it is called in Turkey), and *Muharrem Bayramı*.

BAYRAM KAVURMASI

CELEBRATION LAMB

100 g (3½ oz) lard
1 kg (2 lb 3 oz) hogget (see note), cut into 1 cm (½ inch) cubes
1 large brown onion, peeled and grated, juice reserved
1 tablespoon freshly ground black pepper
2 teaspoons dried oregano
pinch of ground cinnamon
40 g (1½ oz) butter, chopped or melted
Shepherd salad (see page 139), to serve
Turkish bread (see page 50), to serve

In a large heavy-based saucepan, melt the lard over a high heat. Working in batches, fry the meat until browned all over — about 4–5 minutes each batch.

Return all the meat and any juices to the pan. Add the onion and its juice and mix through. Bring to the boil, then turn the heat down to low. Stir the pepper, oregano and cinnamon through. Cover and simmer for about 1 hour, or until the meat is tender and most of the juices have evaporated.

Dot or drizzle the butter over, then put the lid back on. Allow to rest for 10 minutes before serving.

Serve with shepherd salad and Turkish bread.

SERVES 8

NOTE

A hogget is a lamb that is over one year of age. Hogget is lovely in stews. As an alternative you can use lamb in this recipe; being a more tender meat, it won't take quite as long to cook.

Yuuuummmmmm. The Grand Bazaar.

We're not quite sure how these kebabs got their name, but what we do know for certain is that Turks love their kebabs, especially when cooked over charcoal! A haci *is someone who has made the* haj *— the traditional pilgrimage to Mecca. It's almost worth journeying to Turkey just to enjoy these beautiful kebabs.*

HACI OSMAN KEBABI

PILGRIM LAMB KEBABS

1 kg (2 lb 3 oz) boned lamb leg, lightly trimmed of excess fat, then sliced into long, thin strips
2 white onions, peeled and grated
2 tablespoons tomato paste (concentrated purée)
3 garlic cloves, crushed
1 tablespoon cumin seeds, toasted and ground (see note)
1 tablespoon pul biber (see note, page 18)
juice of ½ lemon
125 ml (4 fl oz/½ cup) olive oil
Mint salad (see page 136), to serve
warm Turkish bread (see page 50), to serve

Put the lamb, onion, tomato paste, garlic, cumin, pul biber, lemon juice and olive oil in a large non-metallic bowl. Season with sea salt and freshly ground black pepper and mix together well. Cover and marinate in the refrigerator for 4–5 hours, or overnight if you have time.

Fire up your barbecue to a high heat. If using wooden skewers, soak them in cold water for 20 minutes so they don't scorch on the barbecue.

Thread the lamb onto the skewers, then cook on the barbecue grill bars for 2–3 minutes on each side, or until done to your liking. Remove from the heat and allow to rest for a few minutes.

Serve warm, with mint salad and warm Turkish bread.

SERVES 6–8

NOTE

Freshly toasted and ground cumin seeds add wonderful flavour to dishes. To toast cumin seeds, tip them into a small frying pan and lightly fry them over medium heat for a minute or two, until they smell fragrant, shaking the pan often to toss the seeds around so they don't burn. Then just grind them to a powder using a mortar and pestle (a fabulous kitchen tool — everyone should have one!), or a spice grinder.

You would eat this lovely moussaka for dinner, with salad and bread. It tastes amazing the next day as well. It's a great dinner party dish, as you can prepare it ahead and then sit and enjoy the company of your guests as dinner is baking.

If you like, you can bake the moussaka in your wood-fired oven.

PATLICANLI MUSAKKA

EGGPLANT MOUSSAKA

4 eggplants (aubergines)
sunflower oil, for shallow-frying
60 ml (2 fl oz/¼ cup) olive oil
1 large brown onion, diced
500 g (1 lb 2 oz) minced (ground) beef
2 tablespoons tomato paste (concentrated purée)
30 g (1 oz/1 cup) finely chopped flat-leaf (Italian) parsley
3 tomatoes, sliced
Turkish bread (see page 50), to serve
Radish and watercress salad (see page 73), to serve

Preheat the oven to 180°C (350°F).

Slice the eggplants into rounds about 1 cm (½ inch) thick. Heat about 2.5 cm (1 inch) of sunflower oil in a large heavy-based frying pan, over a medium–high heat. Working in batches, lightly fry the eggplant for about 2 minutes on each side, or until just turning golden. Remove and set aside.

In the same pan, heat the olive oil over a medium heat, then fry the onion until soft, about 6–8 minutes.

Add the beef, tomato paste and half the parsley. Season with sea salt and freshly ground black pepper and mix together for a few minutes until completely warmed through.

Take a deep baking dish, about 35 cm (14 inches) long and 25 cm (10 inches) wide. Line the bottom with a layer of eggplant slices, then add a layer of the beef mixture. Now add another layer of eggplant, and another layer of the beef. Continue layering until all the ingredients are used, finishing with a layer of eggplant. Now arrange the tomato rounds on top and sprinkle with the remaining parsley.

Cover with foil and bake for 30 minutes, or until the eggplant is soft. Remove from the oven and leave to rest for 45 minutes, or up to 1 hour.

Cut the moussaka into squares and serve with Turkish bread and radish and watercress salad.

SERVES 6

Turkish bellies on fire.

Turks love to use their *güveç*. Traditionally these terracotta pots are about 30 cm (12 inches) wide and about 30 cm (12 inches) deep. They can go in a wood-fired oven or an electric one, or sit on the stovetop.

Turks love to eat lamb in spring, and in summer, they eat sheep (which, after the first year, is known as hogget), and then in winter they love mutton. Hogget and mutton can be stewed for a long time, and both are very, very tasty. If you can only get lamb, please be sure to reduce the cooking period to your liking.

KUZU GÜVEÇ
LAMB CASSEROLE

40 g (1½ oz) butter
500 g (1 lb 2 oz) hogget, diced
10 French shallots, peeled
2 large tomatoes, sliced
200 g (7 oz) long green
    chillies, sliced
30 g (1 oz/1 cup) chopped
    flat-leaf (Italian) parsley
Burghul pilaf (see page 143) or
    steamed white rice, to serve

In a flameproof terracotta pot, or heavy-based casserole dish, melt the butter. Place all the meat in the pan, then the shallots. Arrange the tomato slices over the top, then the sliced chillies. Season with sea salt and freshly ground black pepper.

Pour 60 ml (2 fl oz/¼ cup) water over, sprinkle with the parsley and put the lid on. Cook over a low heat until the meat is ready to melt in your mouth and make you smile, about 1½ hours.

Serve with burghul pilaf or steamed white rice — or if you are too lazy to cook these, with just a crust of bread!

This casserole will be even tastier the next day.

SERVES 4

İNCİRLİ KUZU YAHNİSİ

SHOULDER LAMB CHOPS WITH FIGS

500 g (1 lb 2 oz) dried figs
1 kg (2 lb 3 oz) lamb shoulder
  chops, cut in half
50 g (1¾ oz/⅓ cup) plain
  (all-purpose) flour
80 ml (2½ fl oz/⅓ cup) vegetable oil
1 kg (2 lb 3 oz) large white onions,
  roughly sliced
60 g (2 oz/¼ cup) tomato paste
  (concentrated purée)
500 ml (17 fl oz/2 cups) water or
  vegetable stock (I usually just use
  water, as the lamb chops are so
  flavoursome)
2–3 tablespoons ground allspice,
  to taste
10 bay leaves
Burghul pilaf (see page 143),
  to serve

Preheat the oven to 180°C (350°F).

Soak the figs in 250 ml (8½ fl oz/1 cup) hot water for 10 minutes.

Dust the chops with the flour. Heat the vegetable oil in a large frying pan over a high heat. Working in two batches, fry the chops until well browned, about 2–3 minutes on each side. Arrange the chops in a large baking dish.

Add the onion, tomato paste and water or stock to the hot frying pan. Stir in the allspice, then add the bay leaves and season with sea salt and freshly ground black pepper. Strain the figs and pour their soaking liquid into the mixture. Stir well and warm through for a couple of minutes over a medium heat.

Roughly chop the figs and scatter them over the lamb. Pour the onion mixture over the top. Cover with foil and bake for 1½ hours, or until the lamb is tender.

Serve with burghul pilaf.

SERVES 6–8

Karaköy, one of the oldest districts of Istanbul.

ETLİ BEZELYE

PEAS WITH LAMB

60 ml (2 fl oz/¼ cup) olive oil
2 brown onions, diced
250 g (9 oz) lamb backstraps or
    loin fillets, chopped into 1 cm
    (½ inch) cubes
3 tomatoes, diced
500 g (1 lb 2 oz/3¼ cups) freshly
    shelled peas
1 tablespoon sugar
60 g (2 oz/1 cup) chopped dill
crusty bread or Rice pilaf
    (see Chicken pilaf note on
    page 151), to serve

Heat the olive oil in a large heavy-based saucepan over a medium heat. Fry the onion for 6–8 minutes, until soft. Add the lamb and brown well.

Stir in the tomato, peas, sugar and 250 ml (8½ fl oz/1 cup) water. Season with sea salt and freshly ground black pepper.

Turn the heat down to low. Cover and cook until the lamb is tender, about 20 minutes.

Sprinkle with the dill and serve with crusty bread or rice pilaf.

SERVES 4

This is my childhood favourite. I used to beg my mum to make it for me all the time, when cauliflower was in season.

KARNIBAHAR OTURTMASI
CAULIFLOWER WITH MINCED LAMB

1 cauliflower, cut into florets
juice of ½ lemon
250 ml (8½ fl oz/1 cup) olive oil
1 large onion, diced
500 g (1 lb 2 oz) tomatoes, diced
2 long green chillies, diced
30 g (1 oz/1 cup) finely chopped
    flat-leaf (Italian) parsley, plus extra
    to garnish
250 g (9 oz) minced (ground) lamb
500 ml (17 fl oz/2 cups) sunflower oil
50 g (1¾ oz/⅓ cup) plain
    (all-purpose) flour
2 free-range eggs, whisked
500 g (1 lb 2 oz/2 cups) Garlic
    yoghurt (see page 82),
    to serve
Turkish bread (see page 50),
    to serve

Put the cauliflower florets in a large saucepan. Add 3 litres (101 fl oz/ 12 cups) water, the lemon juice and a pinch of sea salt. Bring to the boil, then leave to boil for 10–15 minutes, or until the cauliflower is just tender. Drain while hot, shaking off the excess water.

Meanwhile, in a frying pan, heat the olive oil over a medium heat, then fry the onion for 6–8 minutes, until soft. Add the tomato, chilli, parsley and lamb and season with sea salt and freshly ground black pepper. Cook, stirring, for about 5 minutes, until the lamb is cooked.

Heat the sunflower oil in a frying pan over a medium heat. Working in batches, take each cauliflower floret and roll it in the flour, dip in the egg, then quickly fry in the hot oil until golden. Remove and drain on paper towel while cooking the remaining cauliflower.

Pile all the cauliflower onto a platter or serving plates. Spoon the lamb mixture over the top. Add a good dollop of the garlic yoghurt and sprinkle with a little extra parsley. Serve hot, with Turkish bread.

SERVES 8

The view from my room in Istanbul, below Galata Tower.

If you have time, you can marinate the lamb in the yoghurt and spices for a few hours or overnight, but it will still be very delicious if you wish to cook it straight away.

This dish is wonderful served with Burghul pilaf (see page 143), Smoked eggplant dip (see page 135) or Mint salad (see page 136) — or all three if you wish! Let the feast begin.

YOĞURTLU KİMYONLU KUZU

LAMB SHOULDER COOKED IN YOGHURT & CUMIN SEEDS

3 tablespoons cumin seeds, toasted (see note, page 173)
1 tablespoon pul biber (see note, page 18)
2 tablespoons sea salt
1 tablespoon freshly ground black pepper
1–1.5 kg (2 lb 3 oz–3 lb 5 oz) lamb shoulder, boned and rolled, lightly trimmed of excess fat
250 g (9 oz/1 cup) plain (Greek-style) yoghurt
80 ml (2½ fl oz/⅓ cup) olive oil
flat-leaf (Italian) parsley, to garnish

Preheat the oven to 180°C (350°F), or fire up a wood-fired oven or a hooded barbecue to a medium heat.

Mix together the cumin seeds, pul biber, salt and pepper. Rub the lamb with the yoghurt, then rub the spice mix in, so it all sticks onto the lamb.

Wrap the lamb in foil and bake for 2 hours, or until it is meltingly tender and cooked to your heart's desire. Remove the lamb from the oven and allow to rest for 30 minutes.

Pull the meat apart and pile it onto a platter. Garnish with parsley and serve with your choice of side dishes.

SERVES 6–8

TAZE KUZU ETİ

SPRING LAMB WITH TOMATOES

60 g (2 oz) butter
1 kg (2 lb 3 oz) lamb fillets,
    diced into 2 cm (¾ inch) chunks
3 vine-ripened tomatoes, peeled
    (see note) and diced
15 g (½ oz/½ cup) finely chopped
    flat-leaf (Italian) parsley
8 spring onions (scallions),
    finely chopped
crusty bread, to serve

Melt the butter in a large heavy-based saucepan over a medium–high heat. Add the lamb and brown on all sides for a few minutes.

Stir in the tomato and season with sea salt and freshly ground black pepper. Reduce the heat to low, then cover and simmer for 10 minutes, stirring now and then. If the tomato starts catching on the base of the pan, stir in about 125 ml (4 fl oz/½ cup) water. Cook for a further 20 minutes, or until the lamb is tender.

Sprinkle with the parsley and spring onion and serve with yummy crusty bread.

SERVES 4

NOTE

To peel tomatoes, use a sharp knife to cut a cross into the bottom of each tomato. Place in a heatproof bowl and cover with boiling water. Leave for 30 seconds, then transfer to cold water and peel the skin away from the cross.

In Turkey, kebabs are cooked on metal skewers. If you are using wooden skewers, remember to soak them in cold water for at least 20 minutes before putting them on the barbecue, so they don't get scorched.

ŞİŞ TAVUK

CHICKEN ON SKEWERS

1 large white onion, peeled
2 tablespoons tomato paste
  (concentrated purée)
250 g (9 oz/1 cup) plain (Greek-
  style) yoghurt
125 ml (4 fl oz/½ cup) lemon juice
2 garlic cloves, crushed
125 ml (4 fl oz/½ cup) olive oil
1 kg (2 lb 3 oz) boneless, skinless
  chicken thighs
500 g (1 lb 2 oz) vine-ripened
  tomatoes, cut into quarters
300 g (10½ oz) long green chillies
flat bread, to serve
Red onion & sumac salad
  (see page 140), to serve
lemon wedges, to serve

Grate the onion, wrap it up in a piece of muslin (cheesecloth) and squeeze the juices into a large non-metallic bowl. Add the tomato paste, yoghurt, lemon juice, garlic and olive oil. Season with sea salt and freshly ground black pepper and mix together well.

Cut the chicken into 2 cm (¾ inch) chunks. Add to the marinade and gently massage together for a few minutes. Cover and leave to marinate for at least 1 hour in the refrigerator, or longer if you have time.

If you are going to barbecue these beautiful babies, fire up your barbecue and get your coals glowing like ruby embers. If you don't have time for this, heat your grill (broiler) to its highest setting.

Reserve the juices of the marinade. Onto each skewer, spear two pieces of chicken, then one piece of tomato, a whole chilli, then some more chicken, until the skewer is full. Continue making the rest of the kebabs.

Cook the kebabs on the barbecue grill bars (or under the grill) for 3–4 minutes on each side, or until cooked all the way through, brushing them with the marinade juices during cooking. Remove from the heat and allow to rest for a few minutes.

Serve on flat bread, with red onion and sumac salad, and lemon wedges for squeezing over.

SERVES 4

PAPAZ YAHNISI

BEEF YAHNISI

1 kg (2 lb 3 oz) oyster blade
  or other stewing steak,
  cut into 2 cm (¾ inch) chunks
35 g (1¼ oz/¼ cup) plain
  (all-purpose) flour
60 g (2 oz) butter
500 g (1 lb 2 oz) French
  shallots, peeled
5 garlic cloves, peeled
3 tomatoes, diced
1 teaspoon ground allspice
1 teaspoon ground cinnamon
15 g (½ oz/½ cup) finely chopped
  flat-leaf (Italian) parsley
2 tablespoons white vinegar
250 ml (8½ fl oz/1 cup) beef stock
  or water
crusty bread, to serve

Put the beef in a large bowl. Sprinkle with the flour and toss to coat.

Melt the butter in a flameproof casserole dish. Working in batches, cook the beef over a medium–high heat for 4–5 minutes, until beautifully browned all over. Remove to a large bowl.

In the same casserole dish, brown the shallots and garlic cloves.

Return the beef to the casserole dish, then stir in the tomato, spices, parsley, vinegar and stock. Season with sea salt and freshly ground black pepper. Cover and cook over a low heat for 1–1½ hours, or until the beef is beautifully tender.

Serve with crusty bread.

SERVES 8

I met a few characters in this second-hand shop in Istanbul. Sometimes the memory of people is as important as a place.

KAĞITTA LEVREK

SEA BASS BAKED IN PAPER

50 g (1¾ oz) butter
1 onion, diced
2 long green chillies, diced
juice of 1 lemon
2 vine-ripened tomatoes, chopped
4 bay leaves
4 x 125 g (4½ oz) sea bass fillets,
　　or other firm-fleshed white fish,
　　such as barramundi
30 g (1 oz/½ cup) finely chopped dill
Radish & watercress salad
　　(see page 73), to serve
crusty bread, to serve

Preheat the oven to 180°C (350°F).

Melt the butter in a frying pan over a medium heat. Sauté the onion and chilli for 5 minutes, or until soft. Add the lemon juice, tomato and bay leaves. Season with sea salt and freshly ground black pepper and stir for a few minutes, until the tomato starts to soften.

Place the fish fillets on separate sheets of baking paper, making sure each piece of baking paper is large enough to create a parcel for the fish. Spoon the tomato mixture over all the fish and sprinkle with the dill. Fold each sheet of baking paper up into a parcel, sealing them well.

Place the fish parcels on a baking tray and bake for 10–15 minutes, until the fish flakes easily when tested with a fork.

Remove the fish from the parcels and serve on individual plates, with radish and watercress salad and crusty bread.

SERVES 4

I love the charred flavours of barbecued octopus, with this smooth tahini sauce on top. The tahini sauce is also beautiful with barbecued squid or cuttlefish, or a fillet of barbecued fish.

IZGARADA AHTAPOT

BARBECUED OCTOPUS WITH TAHINI SAUCE

1 kg (2 lb 3 oz) octopus, preferably local, cleaned and roughly chopped
60 ml (2 fl oz/¼ cup) olive oil
juice of 1 lemon

TAHINI SAUCE

2 garlic cloves, peeled
2 slices stale bread, crusts removed, torn into pieces
30 g (1 oz/¼ cup) roughly chopped walnuts
3 tablespoons tahini (see note)
3 tablespoons finely chopped flat-leaf (Italian) parsley
1 tablespoon pul biber (see note, page 18)
100 ml (3½ fl oz) lemon juice, or to taste

Combine the octopus, olive oil and lemon juice in a non-metallic bowl. Season with sea salt. Cover and set aside in the refrigerator to marinate for a few hours.

For the tahini sauce, put the garlic cloves in a mortar with the bread and a pinch of sea salt. Add the walnuts and use a pestle to pound everything into a coarse paste. Scrape the paste into a mixing bowl. Now add the tahini, parsley, pul biber and lemon juice, season with sea salt and freshly ground black pepper and mix together well. Add a little water to the sauce to adjust the consistency if you think it should be a little runnier. Set aside.

Fire up your barbecue and bring it to a high heat. Cook the marinated octopus on the barbecue grill bars for 1–2 minutes, or until tender and just cooked through.

Serve hot, with your beautiful tahini sauce.

SERVES 4

NOTE

Popular throughout the Middle East, and widely available from health food stores, tahini is a paste made from toasted sesame seeds. Turkish tahini is often thinner than tahini from other countries. The oil from the sesame seeds tends to separate from the paste and settle on top, so simply stir the oil back into the tahini before using. For a heavenly breakfast, drizzle some tahini and honey over warm toasted Turkish bread (see page 50).

KAĞITTA LÜFER

BARBECUED FISH

2 whole tailor (bluefish), about
    250 g (9 oz) each, or any other
    white-fleshed fish of your liking
2 tomatoes, peeled (see note,
    page 188) and sliced
2 garlic cloves, sliced
2 long green chillies, chopped
1 lemon, peeled, seeded and chopped
15 g (½ oz/½ cup) finely chopped
    flat-leaf (Italian) parsley
2 bay leaves
100 g (3½ oz) butter, chopped
Rocket salad (see page 74), to serve

Fire up your barbecue and bring it to a medium heat.

Clean and gut the fish, then rinse with cold water.

Take two sheets of foil or baking paper, each about 40 cm (16 inches) square, and lay a quarter of the tomato slices on each. Place a fish on top of each. Season each fish with sea salt and freshly ground black pepper, then cover with the remaining tomato slices. Top each fish with the garlic, chilli, lemon, parsley and a bay leaf. Dot with the butter, then wrap up each fish, making airtight parcels.

Place the fish parcels on the barbecue and cook for about 25 minutes, or until the fish flakes easily when tested with a fork.

Serve immediately, with rocket salad.

SERVES 2

BALIKCISI

Another part of my daily life in Ankara: fresh fish!

If you are ever in Turkey, and you visit a balıkçı or seafood restaurant and see them frying mussels, ask for midye tavası — fried mussels in batter with garlic sauce. They are so delicious!

These lemony, garlicky barbecued mussels are wonderful, too.

MİDYE SALATASI

BARBECUED MUSSELS

2 dozen mussels
3 garlic cloves, peeled
1 teaspoon sea salt
30 g (1 oz/1 cup) finely chopped
    flat-leaf (Italian) parsley
2 tablespoons extra virgin olive oil
zest of 1 lemon
80 ml (2½ fl oz/⅓ cup) lemon juice
crusty bread, to serve

Scrub the mussels and remove any hairy beards. Rinse the mussels in cold fresh water, then leave to drain in a colander.

Fire up your barbecue and bring it to a high heat.

Using a mortar and pestle, crush the garlic cloves and salt together. Transfer to a non-metallic bowl, then add the parsley, olive oil, lemon zest and lemon juice and mix together to make a dressing. Set aside.

Place the mussels on the barbecue grill bars, over the flames. Once they have opened, which will take about 3–5 minutes, use a pair of tongs to take them off the barbecue and place them in a serving bowl, discarding any mussels that haven't opened.

Pour the dressing over the hot mussels and serve with crusty bread.

SERVES 4

AFTER DARK

You'd think that with all this eating, Turkish people should be as round as soccer balls — but traditionally all the meals are prepared at home, from a great variety of healthy and natural foods, with minimal preservatives and processing. There is no such thing as 'junk food' in Turkey, and in any case many people spend so much time and energy preparing their food, there is no time to get fat!

At our home, after the evening meal, once the dinner plates were cleared away, we'd chat, play games, watch TV … and enjoy more food.

Out would come the sweets and little savoury treats: bowls of fresh fruits such as peaches, nectarines and grapes in summer, roasted sunflower seeds and chickpeas, cake or pastries, and more tea — lots of tea!

It wasn't only after dinner that we'd get to enjoy some sweet treats, like some biscuits or a nice bit of cake. It was quite usual for visitors to drop in unannounced, and Turkish people are so hospitable that they will never let you leave their house without feeding you. They will also blackmail you into eating more food — they will say, *If you don't eat I will never speak to you again … How can you possibly not eat more food?* They will bring out some sweet and savoury treats and serve you lots of fresh hot tea, until you cannot eat any more.

On a hot summer's night, we might decide to go for a walk. We'd take the nuts and the seeds and the teapot and sit in a park, to enjoy the little nibbles in the fresh air, and meet with many people we love from our neighbourhood.

In Turkey, there is always food to share.

And at the very end of the night, before we'd go to bed, the fire would continue to burn …

GÜLLÜ VE FISTIKLI KEK

PISTACHIO & ROSE PETAL CAKE

150 g (5½ oz) unsalted butter
300 g (10½ oz) caster
    (superfine) sugar
5 free-range eggs
200 g (7 oz/2 cups) finely
    ground pistachio nuts
1 tablespoon baking powder
zest of 1 orange
petals from 4 unsprayed,
    pesticide-free roses
sifted icing (confectioners')
    sugar, or extra ground pistachio
    nuts, for dusting

Preheat the oven to 160°C (320°F). Butter a 27 cm (10¾ inch) springform cake tin.

In a food processor, blend the butter and sugar together, then add the eggs one at a time, blending after each addition. Add the ground pistachios, baking powder and orange zest and blend until just combined.

Pour half the batter into your cake tin. Spread the rose petals over the batter and pour the remaining mixture over them. Bake for 40 minutes, or until a skewer inserted into the middle of the cake comes out clean.

Leave to cool before removing from the tin. Dust with icing sugar or some extra ground pistachios and serve with love.

This cake is best enjoyed the same day it is baked.

SERVES 8–10

Whenever you want tea, it's just around the corner, even late at night.

This is a most traditional Turkish cake. We love it served with *kaymak* — the Turkish version of clotted cream, which is made by simmering milk for a very long time and skimming off the rich, thick, creamy layer that forms on top of the milk. This is done over and over, with each skimmed layer placed on wooden trays on top of each other. It is truly a labour of love, but the end result tastes completely amazing.

If you can't get hold of *kaymak*, we will graciously accept clotted cream or yoghurt to accompany the cake.

YOĞURT TATLISI

YOGHURT CAKE

50 g (1¾ oz) butter
230 g (8 oz/1 cup) caster
  (superfine) sugar
zest of 1 lemon
5 free-range eggs, separated
250 g (9 oz/1 cup) plain
  (Greek-style) yoghurt
335 g (12 oz/2¼ cups) plain
  (all-purpose) flour
2 teaspoons baking powder
pinch of sea salt
½ teaspoon bicarbonate
  of soda (baking soda)
whipped cream or kaymak
  (Turkish clotted cream),
  to serve

SYRUP

230 g (8 oz/1 cup) caster sugar
250 ml (8½ fl oz/1 cup) cold water
1 tablespoon lemon juice

Preheat the oven to 160°C (320°F). Butter and flour a 27 cm (10¾ inch) springform cake tin.

Using an electric mixer, cream the butter, sugar and lemon zest until fluffy. Add the egg yolks, one at a time, mixing after each addition until thoroughly blended. Mix the yoghurt through.

Sift the dry ingredients into a separate bowl, then fold the dry ingredients into the creamed butter mixture.

In a clean bowl, beat the egg whites until stiff, then fold into the batter. Pour the batter into your cake tin and bake for 50–55 minutes, or until a skewer inserted into the middle of the cake comes out clean.

Meanwhile, make the syrup. Put the sugar and water in a saucepan over a medium heat, stirring until the sugar has dissolved. Bring to the boil, add the lemon juice, and keep boiling over a medium heat for 10 minutes. Allow the syrup to cool.

Cool the cake in the tin for 5 minutes, then turn out onto a serving plate. Spoon the cold syrup over the cake, letting it seep slowly into the cake.

Serve warm, cut into thick slices, with whipped cream or kaymak.

SERVES 10

In Australia it is very hard to get hold of fresh morello cherries, which are a sour cherry variety; they are only really sold frozen or preserved. If anyone knows how I can get fresh sour cherries, do let me know! In Turkey they're called *vişne*, and they have a completely different taste and flavour than your ordinary cherries. They are to die for. We make jam from them, we juice them, we make cakes and desserts with them, we make everything you possibly can from them — we just love them.

VİŞNELİ EKMEK

CHERRY BREAD PUDDING

500 g (1 lb 2 oz) morello cherries, pitted (frozen cherries are nicer than the ones sold in jars)

300 g (10½ oz) caster (superfine) sugar

6 slices day-old white bread, each 1 cm (½ inch) thick, crusts trimmed

100 g (3½ oz) butter, melted

kaymak (Turkish clotted cream) or thick (double/heavy) cream, to serve

45 g (1½ oz/½ cup) flaked almonds, lightly toasted

Put the cherries (and their liquid, if using cherries from a jar) in a bowl. Mix the sugar through and set aside.

Heat the grill (broiler) to high. Grill the bread slices on each side for a few minutes, until they turn golden brown. Brush the melted butter over both sides of the bread. Cut into quarters and arrange on individual serving plates.

Put the cherry mixture in a frying pan and gently warm through until the sugar has dissolved.

Spoon the cherry mixture on top of the bread slices. Add a dollop of kaymak or cream, scatter the flaked almonds over and serve warm.

This pudding is also amazing with plain (Greek-style) yoghurt. Guess what, this way you can have your pudding for breakfast!

Afiyet olsun — May you be healthy. To which you may reply, *Elinize sağlık* — Health to your hands.

SERVES 4–6

You could be in a little alleyway on a tiny stool, having the most amazing discussions, solving the world's problems over a cup of tea.

İRMİK TATLISI

SEMOLINA & YOGHURT CAKE

230 g (8 oz/1 cup) caster
(superfine) sugar
185 g (6½ oz/1½ cups) semolina
250 g (9 oz/1 cup) plain (Greek-
style) yoghurt
75 g (2¾ oz/½ cup) plain
(all-purpose) flour
1 tablespoon baking powder
1 vanilla bean, split lengthways,
seeds scraped

SYRUP

690 g (1½ lb/3 cups) caster sugar
625 ml (21 fl oz/2½ cups) cold water
1 tablespoon lemon juice

Preheat the oven to 180°C (350°F).

Mix all the syrup ingredients in a saucepan and bring to the boil.
Reduce the heat and simmer for 10–15 minutes, or until slightly thickened.
Remove from the heat and allow to cool.

Meanwhile, put the sugar, semolina, yoghurt, flour, baking powder and
vanilla seeds in a bowl and mix together. Pour the batter into a 27 cm
(10¾ inch) springform cake tin.

Bake for about 30 minutes, or until a toothpick inserted in the centre
of the cake comes out clean.

As soon as you take the cake out of the oven, pour the cooled syrup
over the top.

This cake is also great the next day — if there is any left over!

SERVES 10

BURMA

WALNUT SPIRAL

450 g (1 lb/3 cups) plain
   (all-purpose) flour, approximately
   (you may need a little extra)
125 ml (4½ fl oz/½ cup) milk
2 tablespoons vegetable oil
2 free-range eggs, lightly beaten
250 g (9 oz) ground walnuts

SYRUP
440 g (15½ oz/2 cups) sugar
250 ml (8½ fl oz/1 cup) cold water
2 tablespoons lemon juice

Mix all the syrup ingredients in a saucepan and bring to the boil. Reduce the heat and simmer for 10–15 minutes, or until slightly thickened. Remove from the heat and allow to cool.

In a large bowl, mix together the flour, milk, vegetable oil, eggs and a pinch of sea salt. Knead for about 10–15 minutes, until the dough feels like your earlobe. Allow to rest for 10–15 minutes.

Meanwhile, preheat the oven to 160°C (320°F).

Take a small walnut-sized piece of dough and roll it out into a circle, until it is paper thin — like filo pastry. Place some of the ground walnuts in the middle of the dough, then roll the circle up into a log. Now take a large, round baking tray and curl your log of dough into a spiral in the middle of the tray. Make more filled rolls and continue to expand the spiral until all the dough and walnuts are used up.

Transfer to the oven and bake for about 40 minutes, until the pastry is golden brown. Remove from the oven, then pour the cold sugar syrup over the hot pastry. Allow to cool, then you're in heaven!

Serve at room temperature, or chilled. Your walnut spiral will keep in an airtight container at room temperature for up to 3 days.

MAKES 1 BIG SPIRAL

Istanbul lives 24/7. Old and new.

When Mum made this dessert when we were children, she would keep the pumpkin seeds, sprinkle them with salt and bake them. After dinner we would sit around and nibble on them. Another example of Turkish mamas not wasting anything.

KABAK TATLISI

PUMPKIN WITH SUGAR & WALNUTS

1 kg (2 lb 3 oz) pumpkin (winter squash), peeled, seeded and cut into bite-sized pieces
60 ml (2 fl oz/¼ cup) hot water
115 g (4 oz/½ cup) caster (superfine) sugar
125 g (4½ oz/1 cup) chopped walnuts

Arrange the pumpkin pieces in a frying pan large enough to hold them all in a single layer. Splash the hot water over the pumpkin and sprinkle with the sugar. Cover and steam over a medium heat for about 10–15 minutes, or until the pumpkin is just soft.

Place in a bowl and serve warm, sprinkled with the walnuts.

SERVES 6–8

This rich dessert is delicious, it's crispy, it's divine. It should be eaten hot, while the cheese is still oozing. In Turkey, it is generally cooked in a wood-fired oven, but of course you can also use an electric or gas oven.

KÜNEFE

SHREDDED PASTRY WITH CHEESE & SUGAR SYRUP

500 g (1 lb 2 oz) kadayıf
(shredded pastry; see note)
250 g (9 oz) unsalted butter, melted
and cooled
400 g (14 oz) unsalted young
cheddar or mozzarella, grated
100 g (3½ oz/1 cup) ground
pistachio nuts

SYRUP

460 g (1 lb/2 cups) caster
(superfine) sugar
375 ml (12½ fl oz/1½ cups) water
2 tablespoons lemon juice

Light a wood-fired oven, or preheat your oven to 180°C (350°F).

Mix all the syrup ingredients in a saucepan and bring to the boil. Reduce the heat and simmer for 10–15 minutes, or until slightly thickened. Remove from the heat and allow to cool.

Meanwhile, place the pastry in a large bowl. Gently loosen the strands with your fingertips. Pour the melted butter over the pastry and mix well with your fingers, to coat all the pastry with butter.

Spread half the pastry in a large baking dish and sprinkle the cheese over the top. Spread the remaining pastry on top, then flatten the pastry down all over. Bake for 30–35 minutes, or until the pastry is golden.

Remove from the oven and pour the cold syrup over the hot pastry. Sprinkle the ground pistachios over and serve immediately.

SERVES 12–16

NOTE

Kadayıf is a kind of filo pastry that has been shredded into fine threads or strands, and looks like a shredded-wheat breakfast cereal. It also goes by the Greek name, *kataifi*, and is available from Middle Eastern and Mediterranean grocery stores.

Karaköy Wharf, Istanbul, gets under your skin. The energy. The people. The love of life. And the fire.

When I was a little girl my mum would make this sweet soup for us, and for our neighbours. She would make it in the morning and the house would be full of amazing smells. She would soak the chickpeas in one pot, and the beans in another pot. She would boil the wheat, chop the nuts, slice the apples, chop the dried apricots, and she would say, 'Darling, we have to have not less than seven ingredients.' So I would sit and count every ingredient to make sure she didn't miss one. She would make a massive big pot of this sweet soup, then leave it on the stove and let it cool. She would put some into little bowls, and my sister and I would deliver them to our neighbours first. Then we would come home to our own bowls ... one, two, three bowls. We would have a little bread and go back for more. Any guest who came to the house would be offered a bowl as well.

This famous sweet Turkish soup has a lot of myths attached to it. One of them is from the time when the great flood was receding. These were the only ingredients left on Noah's Ark, so they came up with this soup. Traditionally it is prepared by women on the tenth day of the Muslim month of *Muharrem*. It is made for the anniversary of İmam Hüseyın, son of Ali, and grandson of the prophet Muhammed.

Every household has their own version of this soup. This is my mama's.

AŞURE
ASURE

110 g (4 oz/½ cup) dried chickpeas
100 g (3½ oz/½ cup) dried white beans
110 g (4 oz/½ cup) whole wheat (available from Middle Eastern grocers and health food shops)
345 g (12 oz/1½ cups) caster (superfine) sugar
1 tablespoon ground cinnamon
½ teaspoon ground allspice
10 dried figs, chopped
10 dried apricots, finely chopped
60 g (2 oz/½ cup) raisins
1 apple, peeled, cored and thinly sliced
60 g (2 oz/½ cup) chopped hazelnuts
60 g (2 oz/½ cup) chopped walnuts

In separate bowls, soak the chickpeas and beans in plenty of cold water overnight. The next day, rinse them off and cook them in separate saucepans of boiling water until soft — about 1–1½ hours for the chickpeas, and about 1 hour for the beans, depending on the variety.

In a large heavy-based saucepan, bring the wheat and 1.75 litres (60 fl oz/7 cups) water to the boil. Add the chickpeas, beans, sugar, spices, figs, apricots, raisins and a pinch of sea salt. Reduce the heat and simmer, uncovered, over a low heat for 45 minutes, or until all the ingredients are well cooked, and the mixture is the consistency of a thick soup. If the mixture thickens too much, you can stir in a little more water. Remove from the heat.

Layer the apple slices on top and sprinkle with the hazelnuts and walnuts. Leave in a cool part of the kitchen and let the soup cool down.

Serve cool or chilled, in individual bowls.

SERVES 10–12

In Turkey, we love our women, and we love naming dishes for their body parts. This is just another one, very sweet.

HANIM GÖBEĞI

LADIES' NAVELS

100 g (3½ oz) butter
pinch of sugar
150 g (5½ oz/1 cup) plain
   (all-purpose) flour
1 tablespoon fine semolina
3 free-range eggs
sunflower oil, for shallow-frying

SYRUP

460 g (1 lb/2 cups) caster
   (superfine) sugar
375 ml (12½ fl oz/1½ cups) water
2 tablespoons lemon juice

Mix all the syrup ingredients in a saucepan and bring to the boil. Reduce the heat and simmer for 10–15 minutes, or until slightly thickened. Remove from the heat and allow to cool.

In another saucepan, put the butter, sugar and a pinch of sea salt. Add 375 ml (12½ fl oz/1½ cups) water and bring to the boil. Gradually add the flour and semolina, stirring constantly for about 5–6 minutes, until the mixture thickens and pulls away from the side of the pan.

Remove the pan from the heat. Add the eggs one at a time, mixing well after each addition.

Transfer the mixture to a bowl, then cover and rest in the refrigerator for at least 40 minutes, or for a few hours if that suits you better.

In a heavy-based frying pan, heat about 2.5 cm (1 inch) of sunflower oil, over a medium heat. Take walnut-sized pieces of the dough and shape them into balls. Slightly flatten each ball, then create a belly button in the middle with your finger. (You can make your own belly buttons!)

Fry the balls in small batches for about 5 minutes, until golden, turning them over halfway through.

Drain on paper towel, then place on a serving tray. Pour the cold sugar syrup over them and serve. Your ladies' navels will keep in an airtight container at room temperature for up to 3 days.

SERVES 8–10

We all need a piece of *baklava* to end our night.

GÜLLÜ KEK

ROSE PETAL CAKE

3 free-range eggs
300 g (10½ oz) caster
   (superfine) sugar
250 ml (8½ fl oz/1 cup) olive oil
125 ml (4 fl oz/½ cup) milk
300 g (10½ oz/2 cups) self-raising
   flour
petals from 4 sweet-smelling
   unsprayed, pesticide-free red roses
140 g (5 oz/1 cup) hazelnuts, roasted
   and skinned (see note, page 43),
   then chopped

Preheat the oven to 170°C (340°F). Butter and flour a 27 cm (10¾ inch) springform cake tin.

Place the eggs and sugar in a bowl. Using an electric mixer, beat well, until fluffy. Add the olive oil and milk and mix well. Gently fold in the flour and rose petals.

Pour the batter into the cake tin and sprinkle with the hazelnuts. Bake for 35–40 minutes, or until a skewer inserted into the middle of the cake comes out clean.

Leave to cool before removing from the tin. This cake is so delicious while it is still warm, but will keep in an airtight container at room temperature for 2–3 days.

SERVES 10

MUHALLEBİLİ KADAYIF TATLISI

SHREDDED PASTRY WITH CUSTARD

500 g (1 lb 2 oz) kadayıf (shredded pastry; see note, page 218)
250 g (9 oz) unsalted butter, melted and cooled, plus extra for greasing
65 g (2¼ oz/½ cup) crushed pistachio nuts, to serve
dried unsprayed rose petals, to garnish (optional)
pomegranate seeds, to garnish (optional)

SUGAR SYRUP

460 g (1 lb/2 cups) caster (superfine) sugar
375 ml (12½ fl oz/1½ cups) water
2 tablespoons lemon juice

MUHALLEBILI

1 litre (34 fl oz/4 cups) milk
250 g (9 oz) caster sugar
60 g (2 oz/½ cup) cornflour (cornstarch)
90 g (3 oz/½ cup) rice flour
1 free-range egg yolk

Mix all the syrup ingredients in a saucepan and bring to the boil. Reduce the heat and simmer for 10–15 minutes, or until slightly thickened. Remove from the heat and allow to cool.

Preheat the oven to 180°C (350°F). Butter a baking tray.

Place the pastry in a large bowl. Gently loosen the strands with your fingertips. Pour the melted butter over the pastry and mix well with your fingers, to coat all the pastry with butter.

Put all the muhallebili ingredients in a saucepan. Whisk together really well, then place over a medium heat. Stirring constantly, cook for about 5–10 minutes, until the mixture thickens into a custard.

Take a small teacup, then take enough of the pastry to fill the bottom of the teacup. Now add a tablespoon of the custard, then cover with enough pastry to reach the rim. Turn the cup out onto the baking tray. Repeat with the remaining pastry and custard.

Bake for 25 minutes, or until the pastry is golden brown. Remove from the oven and pour the cold sugar syrup over them, while they're still nice and hot.

Serve warm, sprinkled with the crushed pistachios, and garnished with dried rose petals and pomegranate seeds if desired.

SERVES 6–8

There is a lot of love and respect for older people in Turkey. We love them for their wisdom. We kiss their hands and lift them to our foreheads.

ÇAYLI VE CEVİZLİ KEK

TEA & WALNUT CAKE

200 g (7 oz/2 cups) walnut halves
3 free-range eggs
280 g (10 oz/1½ cups, lightly packed) dark brown sugar
250 ml (8½ fl oz/1 cup) strong brewed tea
180 g (6½ oz) unsalted butter, melted
1 tablespoon ground cinnamon
300 g (10½ oz/2 cups) self-raising flour

Preheat the oven to 160°C (320°F). Butter and flour a 27 cm (10¾ inch) springform cake tin.

Finely chop half the walnuts, and cut the remaining walnuts into chunks, keeping them separate.

Place the eggs and sugar in a bowl. Using an electric mixer, beat well, until fluffy. Add the tea, melted butter and cinnamon and mix well. Add the flour and finely chopped walnuts and continue mixing well.

Pour the batter into the cake tin, then sprinkle with the walnut chunks. Bake for 35–40 minutes, or until a skewer inserted into the middle of the cake comes out clean.

Leave to cool before removing from the tin. This cake is best enjoyed the same day it is baked.

SERVES 10

TARÇINLI ELMALI POĞAÇA

CINNAMON & APPLE BABIES

300 g (10½ oz/2 cups) self-
raising flour, approximately
(you may need a little extra)
125 g (4½ oz) unsalted butter,
softened
125 ml (4 fl oz/½ cup) olive oil
2 tablespoons plain (Greek-
style) yoghurt
125 g (4½ oz/1 cup) icing
(confectioners') sugar, plus
extra for sprinkling

FILLING

3 apples
1 tablespoon ground cinnamon
115 g (4 oz/½ cup) caster
(superfine) sugar
2 tablespoons sultanas
(golden raisins)
60 g (2 oz/½ cup) chopped walnuts

Put the flour, butter and olive oil in a bowl and mix thoroughly, using your hands. Add the yoghurt and icing sugar. Knead the dough for about 10 minutes, until it feels like your earlobe. If the dough feels too soft, you can add a little more flour. Cover with a damp cloth and allow to rest for 30 minutes.

Meanwhile, preheat the oven to 170°C (340°F).

To make the filling, grate the apples (I prefer to leave the skin on the apples, to give the pastries more texture), then place in a frying pan. Add the cinnamon, sugar and sultanas and cook for a few minutes over a medium heat, mixing well. Add the walnuts and remove from the heat.

Take the dough and break it into walnut-sized pieces. Using your fingertips, spread each piece into a small saucer shape, about 5 cm (2 inches) in diameter.

Put a tablespoon of the filling on one half of the dough and fold the pastry over, to make a half-moon. Pinch the edges together to seal, then place on a baking tray. Repeat with the remaining dough and filling.

Bake for 25 minutes, or until golden brown all over. Remove from the oven and allow to cool slightly, then sprinkle with a little extra icing sugar. Serve warm or cold.

These little babies will keep in an airtight container at room temperature for up to 3 days.

SERVES 10

INDEX

My mum and me.

ABOUT THE AUTHOR

Born in Ankara, Turkey, Sevtap Yüce started cooking when she was seventeen and learned English while working in a patisserie in Sydney. Sevtap also worked for chef Bill Granger before a sea change took her to Angourie in the Northern Rivers of New South Wales.

Beachwood, Sevtap's first restaurant, opened in 1994. The vibrant café is now located in Yamba, where tourists and locals alike delight in her two great passions: cooking and looking after people.

Turkish Fire is Sevtap's third cookbook, following on from the success of her first two titles, *Turkish Flavours* and *Turkish Meze*.

ACKNOWLEDGEMENTS

A big thank you to the people of Turkey, for having the best sense of humour, for giving me a million helping hands, and for turning the impossible into the possible.

To Sally Abrahams, still the best secretary general going around: you rock!

To Robert and Sally Molines: thank you both for your amazing hospitality while I wrote this book, and for making me feel loved and cared for.

To Lisa Dempster of Jac + Jack: thank you for your friendship and for all the beautiful clothes — love you, sister!

To everyone who helped create this book — Fiona Hardie, Sandy Grant, Paul McNally, Mark Campbell, Alicia Taylor, Sarah DeNardi, Hamish Freeman, Klarissa Pfisterer, Katri Hilden, Caroline Jones and Rihana Ries — thank you for your hard work and support.

To all of my wonderful customers: thank you for supporting Beachwood. When you walk through the café doors, you walk into my home.

And finally, to my beautiful, loving, hardworking café staff: I'm so grateful that you are part of my life.

An SBS book

Published in 2015 by Hardie Grant Books

Hardie Grant Books (Australia)
Ground Floor, Building 1
658 Church Street
Richmond, Victoria 3121
www.hardiegrant.com.au

Hardie Grant Books (UK)
5th & 6th Floors
52–54 Southwark Street
London SE1 1UN
www.hardiegrant.co.uk

A Cataloguing-in-Publication entry is available
from the catalogue of the National Library of
Australia at www.nla.gov.au

Turkish Fire
ISBN 978 1 74270 876 8

Publishing Director: Paul McNally
Project Editor: Rihana Ries
Editor: Katri Hilden
Design Manager: Mark Campbell
Designer: Pfisterer + Freeman
Photographer: Alicia Taylor
Stylist: Sarah DeNardi
Recipe Tester: Caroline Jones
Production Manager: Todd Rechner

Colour reproduction by Splitting Image
Colour Studio
Printed and bound in China by 1010 Printing
International Limited

Find this book on
Cooked.
cooked.com.au | cooked.co.uk